Continuous improvement in action – the journey of eight companies

Maeve Gallagher

Sarah Austin

and Sarah Caffyn

CIRCA (Continuous Improvement Research for Competitive Advantage) was a five-year research project at the University of Brighton which investigated the implementation of CI within UK firms. The work was supported by the Department of Trade and Industry and the Engineering and Physical Sciences Research Council.

Maeve Gallagher completed a postgraduate qualification in Occupational Psychology at the Queen's University in Belfast before joining the CIRCA team in 1996. She is now working with European partners to develop guidelines for the management of technology in small to medium-sized enterprises.

Sarah Austin formerly worked at the University of Brighton where she researched new manufacturing technologies in small and medium-sized firms, quality and employee involvement and continuous improvement. She now works in the multi-media industry.

Sarah Caffyn has been researching continuous improvement at the University of Brighton since 1992. Her current interests include the application of CI to new product development processes. She previously worked in the multi-media and publishing industries.

Continuous improvement in action – the journey of eight companies

Maeve Gallagher

Sarah Austin

and Sarah Caffyn

Edited by Maeve Gallagher

KOGAN
PAGE

YOURS TO HAVE AND TO HOLD
BUT NOT TO COPY

First published in 1997

Kogan Page Limited
120 Pentonville Road
London N1 9JN

British Library Cataloguing in Publication Data
A CIP record for this book is available from the British Library.

ISBN 0 7494 2436 2

Typeset by Northern Phototypesetting Co Ltd, Bolton
Printed and bound in Great Britain by Biddles Ltd, Guildford and King's Lynn

Contents

6 CONTENTS

List of Figures

List of Tables

Abbreviations and Glossary

ASRAAM   Advance Short Range Air to Air Missile.

BAe   British Aerospace Limited.

BDA   British Deming Association – association which teaches the principles and practices of quality management as outlined by Dr W Edwards Deming.

BS5750   National standard for quality management systems, introduced in 1979 by the British Standards Institution.

CAP   Competitive Achievement Plan – strategic initiative at Lucas headquarters to assess the potential of their Diesel Systems subsidiary and plan a course of action.

CCF   'Cardiff Customer Focus' is a CI strategy implemented at NPI Cardiff to drive and focus improvement efforts on communicating with customers.

CE   Concurrent Engineering is the integration of product design and manufacturing design aimed at increasing speed of products to market.

CI   Continuous Improvement – an organisation-wide process of focused and sustained incremental innovation.

CIAGs   Continuous Improvement Activity Groups consisted of small groups of employees at BAe Dynamics Division, mainly operators and engineers, who came together outside their normal work activities to generate specific process improvements, disbanding once the problem had been solved.

CIRCA   Continuous Improvement Research for Competitive Advantage – a five-year research project at the University of Brighton (1992–97).

CPA   Corrective and Preventative Action – a system which deals with issues raised by quality 'incidents', for example arising from customer complaints, audit failures, supplier failures, customer returns or production yield problems.

Crosby philosophy   The Crosby philosophy of Quality focuses on the extent to which quality conforms to certain requirements as defined by Philip Crosby, a leading figure in quality management.

cause and effect (or fishbone) diagram   The cause and effect diagram is one of the seven quality tools (see 'seven quality tools') which is used to brainstorm possible causes contributing to a particular problem or defect.

Deming, W E   Dr W Edwards Deming is one of the most prominent names in quality management. One of the central tenets of the Deming 14-point philosophy of management is that quality must be at all levels and across all functions within a company.

Deming cycle   The Deming cycle is one of the quality control tools, introduced by W Edwards Deming to Japan. It is a methodology for improvement in a systematic way and is also known as the PDCA (Plan-Do-Check-Act) cycle.

DQS   Dynamics Quality Strategy is a strategy used by BAe Dynamics to help coordinate and prioritise all the company's continuous improvement activities.

DTI   Department of Trade & Industry.

EFQM   The European Foundation for Quality Management was founded in 1988 by the presidents of 14 companies to stimulate and assist organisations throughout Europe in participating in improvement activities.

EFQM Model   The European Foundation for Quality Management Business Excellence Model is a framework used by companies to assess their performance. There are nine criteria: Customer Satisfaction, People Satisfaction, Impact on Society, Processes, People Management, Policy

	and Strategy, Resources, Leadership and Business Results.
fishbone diagram	The fishbone diagram is one of the 'seven quality tools' used to brainstorm possible causes contributing to a particular problem or defect.
IIP	Investors In People – a British National Standard which encourages organisations to adopt a strategic approach to employee development and is supported by the Training and Enterprise Council.
IIP Award	The Investors In People Award is an accreditation for organisations which have met the National Standard for effective investment in people.
JIT	Just-in-Time is a technique refined in Japan by Toyota as a means of controlling inventory and reducing waste in production.
kaizen	Kaizen is a Japanese word: 'Kaizen means gradual unending improvement, doing "little things" better: setting – and achieving – ever higher standards.'[1]
kanban	A communication tool in the Just-in-Time production and inventory control system.
KPC	Key Performance Criteria – main performance measures by which a company measures its success and progress.
KPS	Kawasaki Production System is based on Just-in-Time, waste elimination and continuous improvement principles to increase productivity and efficiency within manufacturing.
LDS	Lucas Diesel Systems.
LIFE	Little Improvements From Everyone – an employee involvement scheme which encourages input at an individual level. The scheme was devised at Lucas Diesel Systems as part of their Continuous Improvement programme.
MRPII	Manufacturing Resource Planning is a computerized system which integrates the key

---

[1] Imai, 1987.

business processes in a firm.

NPD New Product Development is the process which takes a product from original concept through to full-scale production.

NPI National Provident Institution.

NVQ National Vocational Qualification – a range of competence-based units of training and assessment which can be used to develop and train employees in line with company objectives, and contribute towards Investors In People accreditation.

PAPA Process and Performance Analysis – a reporting system (used at NPI) to help staff control their daily work processes and generate management information for decision-making.

Pareto analysis Pareto analysis is one of the 'seven quality tools' (see 'seven quality tools') used to separate the 'vital few' causes of a problem from the 'trivial many'.

PCB Printed Circuit Board – a circuit board used in the assembly of electronics equipment.

PIPS Process Improvement/Problem-Solving cycle used at Hosiden Besson.

PIT Process Improvement Team – cross-functional teams set up to address specific opportunities for improvement within different processes at Lucas Diesel Systems.

PONC Price Of Non-Conformance – a term coined by the management guru Phillip Crosby which refers to the cost of failure, eg over- or under-production or failing to detect or correct errors.

QIP Quality Improvement Process – a continuous improvement strategy implemented at NPI.

QIT Quality Improvement Team – groups responsible for driving the Quality Improvement Process at NPI.

R&D Research & Development.

RAF Royal Air Force.

SMT Surface Mount Technology.

SPC Statistical Process Control is one of the 'seven

	quality tools' (see 'seven quality tools') used to detect potential problems before they occur, through ongoing monitoring of a process or machine. The technique uses control charts on which the performance of the machine or process is plotted and any atypical variation is investigated and resolved.
SQR	Systems Query Report is a formal process introduced at NPI to raise issues about systems and ensure that a change is consistent across all areas that are affected.
SUK	Schunk UK.
'Seven tools of quality'	The 'seven tools of quality' are a set of simple and long-established techniques for data analysis and quality improvement in operations. The tools were originally assembled by Karou Ishikawa and were used in Japan.
TCA	Teaching Company Associate: the Teaching Company Scheme is a graduate placement programme sponsored by the Department of Trade and Industry.
TQM	'Total Quality Management is typically a company-wide effort seeking to install and make permanent a climate where employees continuously improve their ability to provide on demand products and services that customers will find of particular value.'[2]

[2] Ciampa (1992), p xxi. See also Sashkin and Kiser (1991).

Acknowledgements

Many thanks to the companies which gave their time and provided the information for this book. Thanks also go to all those who have contributed to the research and in particular to Professor John Bessant, Steve Webb, Jane Burnell, John Gilbert, Rebecca Harding, Pauline Nissen and Graham Perrin.

About CIRCA

Continuous Improvement Research for Competitive Advantage (CIRCA) is a research project at the University of Brighton initially sponsored by the Department of Trade and Industry (DTI) and subsequently by the Engineering and Physical Sciences Research Council (EPSRC). It explores the application potential of Continuous Improvement (CI) within companies. Since 1992 CIRCA has been building up a generic model of CI – from initial implementation to becoming an integral part of organisational learning and development.

The project – based on a five-year foundation of academic research, UK and overseas partnerships, and collaboration with more than 100 companies within the UK – has led to a practical understanding of CI success factors. As one output of the research, this casebook charts CI implementation in eight companies with which the CIRCA team has worked.

Introduction

WHAT IS CONTINUOUS IMPROVEMENT?

'Continuous improvement' (CI) is a widely-used phrase which has taken on a variety of meanings, the interpretation of which may differ from one organisation to another. For many people it is a concept synonymous with 'innovation', the continual quest to make things better in products, processes and customer service. For others, it is a core value that lies at the heart of organisational renewal programmes such as Total Quality Management (TQM). CI can also refer to a range of activities aimed at improving processes and productivity, often with a particular aim such as the elimination of waste, and often with application to specific functions, for example the role of Japanese manufacturing techniques in improving efficiency on the shop floor.

The above interpretations of CI, whether as a concept, a value or an initiative, all share a common feature in that they involve high levels of problem-solving. They also have a common objective: regardless of 'what' CI refers to in a company – from high impact strategic programmes to small-scale individual improvements – the 'why?' aspect of CI implementation for an organisation is to help to achieve competitive advantage.

Whilst the quest for continuous improvement has always preoccupied organisations, recent interest can be related to a second dimension – that of *involvement*. Traditional approaches to innovation tend to see this task as belonging to qualified specialists, with an emphasis on major changes. Incremental innovation, when it happens, is attributed to 'learning curve' effects or similar phenomena. But efforts have been made – notably in post-war Japan – to involve a large proportion of the workforce in sustained and targeted incremental problem-solving. The results of this have brought dramatic gains along a variety of performance dimensions and stimulated concern for the widespread implementation of high involvement CI systems.

Here we will define CI as 'an organisation-wide process of focused and sustained incremental innovation' [1]. This interpretation recognises that much innovative activity is not of the 'breakthrough' variety but is incremental in its nature, and involves a high proportion of the workforce. This form of CI can be described as small-step, high-frequency, short cycles of change which have little impact when viewed alone, but which cumulatively can make a significant contribution to performance.

BACKGROUND TO THE CASE STUDIES

The companies represented in the book are of varying size and are at different stages of implementation; as such, they provide some indication of both the range of possible variations on the basic CI theme and the common problems. The contributing companies include large multi-national companies – for example Lucas Diesel Systems – and small businesses, such as the family-owned Fortes Bakery Limited based in West Sussex.

Seven of the cases are in the manufacturing sector, including British Aerospace Dynamics Division, Hosiden Besson Limited, Veeder Root Environmental Systems Limited and Schunk UK Limited. There is one case from the service sector – NPI, a provider of retirement-related products.

The reasons for adopting CI vary from one organisation to another, but all have experienced pressure from external sources, including increased competition, changes in the market and changes in customer demands. Some have undergone periods of uncertainty due to organisational changes such as takeover, merger or downsizing, while others have had to deal with cultural problems such as internal rivalry, poor communication, ineffective management and demotivated employees.

Each of the cases will be described in terms of company background with a detailed account of the approach to CI implementation and a review of the key points to be learned from the study. The core text of the cases demonstrates the wide range of CI techniques and philosophies which can be applied and some of the individual approaches taken by different companies. The reviews will pull out some of the key themes of each case, highlight the benefits gained, and comment on the impact and value of CI to the company.

The concluding chapter of the book draws out some of the general themes and lessons learned, along with more general comments on implementation. For the CI practitioner this book offers some valuable lessons for implementation and advance warning of some of the pitfalls to be avoided. Other readers will gain an understanding of CI in action based on the experience of a range of companies. A more extended discussion of the principles of CI can be found in the paper 'High-involvement innovation through continuous improvement' [1].

The rest of the introduction will cover some of the key issues relating to CI, including the history of CI, examples of what can be achieved by its application, and some of the key success factors, as well as barriers to implementation.

THE HISTORY OF CI

The historical roots of CI can be traced to companies in the UK and US as far back as the nineteenth century [2]. The very effective Training Within Industry (TWI) service set up by the US government in 1940 to quickly boost industrial output and productivity on a national scale included Job Methods Training, a programme designed to teach supervisors the importance of and the techniques for achieving continuous methods improvement [3].

In fact, many of the ideas underlying so-called 'Japanese management' have their roots in US management philosophy and practice. They were introduced into Japan after the Second World War by US management experts like W Edwards Deming, Joseph Juran and Dr Lillian Gilbreth, and via massive management training programmes (which included the TWI courses) initiated by the US occupation forces [3].

Over the following years, the Japanese adapted and developed these ideas. The term quality control, originally used to refer specifically to quality control of the manufacturing process, acquired a much broader meaning as it grew into a management tool for *kaizen*, or ongoing improvement involving everyone [4]. Impressed by Japanese economic success, Western companies tried to emulate practices they saw in Japan, a prime example being the attempts to set up Quality Circles during the late 1970s and early 1980s, many of which failed. This lack of success stemmed from a misunderstanding of the nature of the Japanese Total Quality Control movement, in which Quality Control Circles were just one element in a company-wide drive towards quality improvement and change [5]. Later, Total Quality Management programmes, which recognised the need for an all-encompassing approach, became popular in the West.

TQM is just one of several routes down which companies have journeyed to arrive at CI. For example, in some cases CI has followed the adoption of 'Japanese manufacturing techniques' such as 'Just-In-Time'. In recent times some companies, which see knowledge as the basis for competition, have started to try and develop 'learning organisations' by increasing involvement in innovative problem-solving [1].

WHY IS CI IMPORTANT?

☐   There is now substantial evidence to support the view that innovation matters as a key strategic resource.

☐   A growing number of organisations, world-wide and in the UK, are adopting CI as a way to harness the creativity of employees and gain competitive advantage in the marketplace.

☐   Although the objective may seem straightforward, putting it into effect is much more complicated. On the evidence of a number of studies, as well as examples of CI in practice, it seems that successful implementation involves a core commitment and long-term investment from the organisation. However, there is evidence that implementation is worth the effort, and of those firms who have implemented CI a significant number have reported achieving a number of benefits from doing so.

☐ A survey carried out in the UK [6] (as part of a larger investigation into CI activities in Europe and Australia) found that as many as 89 per cent of the 142 firms taking part claimed that CI had made an impact on at least one performance indicator, including productivity, manufacturing quality and delivery performance.

BENEFITS OF CI

A major attraction of CI is that it does not have to involve large capital investment, because at the heart of the concept is the belief that positive change occurs through investing in people – 'with every pair of hands comes a free brain'! Therefore, implementation, though not cost-free, can be a low-cost investment, which makes it accessible for all types of organisations, including small-scale enterprises. CI can result in a number of tangible benefits, for example:

☐ Increased profitability through reducing internal costs.

☐ Greater efficiency and better use of time.

☐ Maximised use of resources (human, financial and equipment).

☐ Improved processes leading to increased customer satisfaction.

☐ Increased skill level and flexibility of employees.

Tangible outcomes

The tangible benefits are often linked to financial outcomes, such as reduction of costs, reductions in waste and increased profit; as such, they are quantifiable and can be used to assess the impact of the CI programme. However, it is a mistake to judge the success of CI on financial measures alone, as there are a number of benefits which may not be evident in the short term but are important indicators of the extent to which change has taken root and helped the company to evolve.

Intangible benefits

Intangible benefits include those factors which contribute to the improvement process but cannot be quantified. Examples of some of the intangible benefits are listed below:

☐ Improved relationships – such as the breakdown of internal barriers between different levels and functions.

☐ Improved external partnerships – with customers and suppliers.

☐ Enhanced communication and cooperation across levels and functions.

☐ Increased employee morale and job satisfaction.

A successful CI programme will aim to achieve both tangible and intangible outcomes which contribute to a change in culture as well as a change in processes and work practice. For example, the introduction of a new system should be evaluated on the extent to which it contributes to individual learning and improved communication as well as the extent to which it meets financial targets. This is the difference between a CI programme which incorporates long-term planning and objectives and one which is focused on making quick impact short-term changes. Long-term planning with interim targets has been identified as a factor contributing to successful implementation of CI. However, there is no one single easy route to successful application and there are a number of barriers which companies have encountered when trying to follow a prescribed philosophy or methodology, without taking internal factors into account.

BARRIERS TO CI IMPLEMENTATION

Despite its attractions, evidence suggests that CI often fails to take root or deliver what it seems to promise. In many cases, this is due to a problem with the design and management of CI systems [7]. There is no single formula for success which can be applied to all situations, and contingent factors such as the company culture, structure and background need to be taken into account when planning implementation.

Nevertheless, there do appear to be some difficulties associated with implementation, which CI practitioners frequently come up against. The following examples illustrate some of the issues which are often overlooked when implementing CI:

- **Narrow focus of CI initiative** – limiting the impact to local areas which do not offer people from other departments the opportunity to get involved.

- **Superficial implementation** – such as buying in expertise and technology, or giving glossy presentations or training programmes, without taking into account the underlying behaviours which need to be changed or developed.

- **Copying programmes used by other organisations** without taking the local context into account, for example, company culture, educational level of workforce or the reasons for CI implementation.

- **Not changing the emphasis of the CI programme** to rejuvenate enthusiasm, refocus attention and sustain the momentum.

- **Aligning CI to specific activities**, in selected areas of the company, which can lead to very localised improvements that may have a limited impact on the overall aims of the company.

- **Introducing an overly complex CI programme** that incorporates a number of philosophies and projects, which can prove difficult to coordinate and may quickly fizzle out as people start to suffer from initiative overload.

- **Not using effective measurement** and feedback mechanisms to monitor and evaluate the success of the programme.

- **Company culture** – lack of time, resistance to change and fear of the unknown. Or trying to force change on people at a pace that is too fast, or without first gaining their support and trust.

- **Lack of management commitment** or active involvement, including little or no understanding of what the change process involves or the role they are expected to play in the process.

The above examples illustrate how CI can fail to lead to improvement as a result of poor planning and overlooking the role played by employees in bringing about change.

FACTORS IN CI IMPLEMENTATION

While it is something of a cliché to talk of CI as 'a journey and not a destination', it might be helpful at this point to highlight a few important points which can often be overlooked when planning to introduce CI to the company.

☐ It should be stressed that CI is not a single event, nor is it a set of tools and techniques. Rather, it is a long-term learning process which is dynamic and will go through a number of phases and changes [1].

☐ Company objectives provide a framework for driving change to help ensure that CI activity is directed towards organisational goals.

☐ There will also need to be mechanisms to encourage and facilitate individual and group involvement at all levels.

The latter points stem from the need for a CI initiative to have an impact on the overall business aims of the company and gain the support and commitment of people at all levels.

The cases in this book illustrate the range of approaches companies take to ensure that the programme incorporates these key characteristics. For example, Lucas Diesel Systems and Hosiden Besson Ltd employed full-time CI engineers to manage improvement initiatives which encourage cross-functional team working as well as individual involvement. The insurance company NPI and British Aerospace Dynamics Division manage CI as a series of phases moving from operational to strategic initiatives. Veeder Root Environmental Systems manage CI as an ongoing process of incremental improvement with quick impact and high visibility in order to sustain momentum and involvement.

DEVELOPMENT OF CI

The above examples illustrate some of the different approaches which can be taken to CI. As has been noted, there is no one single 'suit all' approach to implementation, but there are a number of guidelines which illustrate how CI can move from the early stages of implementation to a strategically-managed programme with high involvement at all levels.

In the early stages of development, efforts can be taken up with the basics of putting together a workable programme which integrates the generation of ideas with their implementation. This may also include the development of a system to ensure that effort is recognised. Other developments in the early stages of the programme may include setting in place some mechanism to measure and record the improvements as well as a means of identifying targets in the short and long term to help sustain momentum and keep people focused and motivated.

Not surprisingly, many programmes run aground in the early stages. However, some persist and begin to link their CI skills with the needs of the overall business strategy. This requires learning new skills around monitoring and measuring processes – but the results will have more strategic impact. Further down the road is the possibility of self-directed CI, in which the organisation moves towards a devolved form of innovation with high levels of participation.

Although designing and managing the system are integral to the development and success of the CI programme, the key factor in changing an organisation, which has been identified by researchers and practitioners alike, is changing the role played by the people in the organisation.

CHANGING THE ORGANISATION THROUGH THE PEOPLE

An approach which many companies have found helpful is to look at CI not as a set of activities but as a suite of behaviours which evolve over time within an organisation.

The behaviours can be broadly defined under the following themes:

☐ **Understanding** – employees demonstrate awareness and understanding of the organisation's aims and objectives and how they could contribute towards these.

☐ **Strategic focus** – individuals and groups use the organisation's strategic goals and objectives to focus and prioritise their improvement activities.

☐ **Development of CI** – the 'enablers' (ie training, teamwork, tools, methodologies, etc) used to encourage involvement in CI are monitored and developed.

☐ **Consistency** – ongoing assessment ensures that the organisation's structure, systems and procedures, and the approach and mechanisms used to encourage CI, consistently reinforce and support each other.

☐ **Leadership** – managers at all levels display active commitment to, and leadership of, CI.

☐ **Involvement** – throughout the organisation people engage proactively in incremental improvement.

☐ **Cross-boundary working** – there is effective working across internal and external divisions at all levels.

☐ **Learning** – people learn from their own and others' experiences, both positive and negative.

☐ **Spread of knowledge** – the organisation ensures that the learning of individuals and groups is captured, shared with others, and applied where appropriate.

☐ **Shared beliefs** – people are guided by a shared set of cultural values underpinning CI as they go about their everyday work.

New behavioural norms evolve gradually. In most situations, be it in an organisation or a national population, there are usually a limited number of trendsetters who adopt new social conventions and patterns of behaviour ahead of the majority [8]. In the early stages people may enact the behaviour self-consciously, practising it, reminding themselves what to do (like someone learning to drive a car): it is only by repeating it over and over again that it becomes an ingrained, automatic way of behaving.

Changing people's behaviour is not easy, and it can take a long time. Research has shown that companies may pass through several development stages of CI as they move towards a situation where the vast majority of the organisation is actively engaged in making improvements which, taken cumulatively, have a significant impact on business goals.

Adopting a behavioural approach to CI has several advantages. First, the behaviours are described in a way which is generic; that is, they are not organisation-specific, and can be applied to every setting. Secondly, the behaviours indicate to companies what they need to focus on in order to achieve the levels of involvement necessary for successful CI.

These behaviours represent a new way of working, and a change in attitude, which require firms to break out of their old mindsets and find ways to encourage their people to adopt the new behaviours. This is not easy, involving as it does the unlearning of old behaviours and the practising new ones until they become routine. Despite the difficulties, there are still many actions a company can take to help bring about the desired change.

ENABLING MECHANISMS

There are a number of enablers, or 'interventions', which can be used to encourage the development of these behaviours and help the company to progress through the different stages of CI proficiency. Examples include the use of training to develop new skills and attitudes, or the use of problem-solving methodologies, facilitators and recognition systems to encourage people to generate and implement ideas.

The 'journey' towards improvement taken by each organisation will be influenced by the types of issue they wish to address. The following examples extracted from the book illustrate different approaches to change and demonstrate some of the enablers used to help foster the 'CI behaviours'.

☐ **Improving efficiency and reducing costs** – In manufacturing settings such as Schunk UK Limited, British Aerospace (BAe) and Lucas Diesel Systems, the initial focus of attention was to improve internal systems and processes. The companies originally focused on improving productivity and reducing wastage in operations through the adoption of techniques such as Just-in-Time (JIT) and, in the case of BAe, a formal waste elimination programme. The companies encouraged cultural change by introducing support mechanisms and deploying staff to encourage team working and cross-functional communication. The focus of improvement was gradually rolled out to incorporate other sections within the organisation and the emphasis moved from operational to business-focused improvements. BAe spread the impact of the waste elimination programme by aiming to eliminate waste from the supply chain as a joint initiative with some of their suppliers.

☐ **Encouraging involvement** – some of the companies engaged full-time CI engineers to lead and support the improvement process, for example at Hosiden Besson Limited in East Sussex. The company set up two enabling mechanisms to encourage participation, one directed at team activity and the other at encouraging individual involvement. The idea for the latter was adapted from the 'Little Improvements From Everyone' (LIFE) scheme developed by Lucas Diesel Systems, which demonstrates the value of learning from the success of others! At Veeder Root Environmental Systems, in Leicestershire, there is no formal system to drive activities and yet CI happens on an ongoing basis through the improvement teams. This is largely due to the support given by the site director, who has a very 'hands on' approach to managing and implementing CI.

☐ **Management commitment** – leadership and commitment have been identified as key factors in the successful implementation of CI. All of the case firms have managers who display an active commitment to CI. This is demonstrated by investing resources and time in the programme, for example at TM Products. At Fortes Bakery it was recognised that the company needed to encourage a more visible and active form of leadership. The management undertook training in leadership and facilitation skills, in order to lead by example and demonstrate that their first commitment to changing the culture was to change their own behaviour.

□ **Strategic focus** – the change process at NPI aimed to improve customer satisfaction. This was achieved by adopting a planned approach to training and developing the skills of the employees. As a result, employees had increased control over their work and more contact with customers, which helped to improve job satisfaction. The strategic aim of exceeding customer requirements was supported by encouraging employees to have a process approach to change. The introduction of a new employee suggestion and recognition scheme helped to capture any improvement ideas relating to both incremental and strategic changes.

□ **Implementing CI at a pace that suits the company culture** – at Lucas Diesel Systems the change was well paced and reflective, which allowed the company to assess the value of different aspects of the programme before rolling out the initiative to have a wider impact. At BAe and NPI a phased approach to change was adopted. NPI concentrated first on improving efficiency within operations and then developed their programme to incorporate the achievement of more strategic objectives. TM Products implemented a number of systems and initiatives aimed at dealing with current procedural and cultural problems in order to help the company to evolve into the kind of organisation it wanted to be.

□ **Using effective means of communication** – electronic mail systems are increasingly being used as a means of communication in organisations. This has proved a successful medium for transmitting information at both NPI and Veeder Root. Regular meetings and team briefings are among the most common forms of communication which, when they are an integral part of the work process, help ensure that information is timely and appropriate for the recipient. Forms of communication which are *ad hoc* or parallel to daily working are more difficult to implement successfully, and this theme will be explored in more detail throughout the book.

These are just some of the examples of how the change process was managed in different situations. Other interesting features to note from the cases include the development of management skills at Fortes Bakery and the application of CI to an office environment at NPI in Cardiff. The programme at NPI has made significant progress in improving both customer satisfaction and employee motivation.

COMMON THEMES

A number of themes occur regularly throughout the book including, among others, teamworking, recognition, leadership, involvement and management.

The concluding chapter will draw out some of the main learning points from the cases, and discuss the implications of some of the key issues. It will also pull together some of the examples of good practice and difficulties encountered which emerge from the studies, as well as examining trends in implementation and how they contribute to a greater understanding of CI in action.

While the cases provide good examples of some of the factors contributing to successful CI and benefits companies have gained from it, they also show how the journey to improvement is characterised by wrong turnings and changes in direction – demonstrating the importance of having a good road map to guide what is, in effect, an iterative learning process. Ultimately, the companies which sustain and develop CI are the ones which are capable of learning and evolving and adapting to the challenges which may arise.

Case 1
BRITISH AEROSPACE DEFENCE DYNAMICS LIMITED

British Aerospace Defence Dynamics Limited is a consolidation of all guided weapons systems business for BAe, formed in 1988 from three previously separate companies on eight sites.

OVERVIEW OF CASE

In the late 1970s, British Aerospace Defence Limited faced few competitive challenges, with consistently high levels of demand and healthy profits and margins. Moving into the 1980s, two key external changes occurred which posed a serious threat to the organisation's competitive performance: first, the government instigated an overhaul of BAe's pricing system and secondly, the Cold War drew to an end. BAe formed its Dynamics subsidiary and responded to shifts in the competitive environment by introducing a series of improvement programmes aimed at eliminating inefficiencies, bringing about further reductions in its cost base and, ultimately, increasing competitiveness.

Following an early initiative to bring in greater project control, improvement efforts started in earnest around 1990 with an overhaul of the production operations and continued through a chain of programmes in related system and design areas. In the mid-1990s an ambitious, company-wide improvement programme was introduced, integrating many elements of the preceding, localised change initiatives.

BACKGROUND

As part of the drive to cut public spending under the Thatcher administration, cost-plus pricing was abolished in 1985 in favour of fixed-price and target-price systems. Under the latter, the price incorporated a sliding scale of the amount of profit that the company could earn from the contract depending on how near the actual costs were to meeting the original target price. The outcome was the creation of a much tougher, more competitive environment in which inefficiencies could no longer be tolerated.

The impact of these governmental changes was further compounded by the contraction in the world-wide defence equipment market in the late 1980s, as the end of the Cold War signalled an improvement in East–West relations. BAe Defence Limited was effectively being squeezed from two angles.

Drastic change was required if the company was to survive and become more competitive. More specifically, it needed to get to grips with its cost base and inefficiencies to halt the squeeze on profit margins. The company responded in two ways. First, it instigated a major rationalisation programme, which continued into the first half of the 1990s. Secondly, it consolidated to form Dynamics.

RATIONALISATION

BAe Defence had long operated a system of cost-plus pricing, whereby any additional project costs which had not been anticipated at the outset or were incurred due to problems and errors could simply be passed on to the customer by increasing the price. Thus projects could accommodate any expenditure without having an adverse affect on profit margins. The downside of such a system was that it created, and maintained, widespread inefficiencies and led to an enormous amount of wastage, particularly with respect to the product introduction cycle.

Prior to the formation of BAe Dynamics, each site suffered the common problems of excess capacity and declining workloads, highlighting the company's inability to survive in its existing state. The merger into Dynamics created the further problem of duplicated resources.

Whilst Dynamics was given no guarantee of survival, the new management team was presented with the opportunity to turn the business around. To this end, a new business strategy was developed by the Dynamics management, central to which was the need to refocus on core business. The strategy incorporated the following objectives:

- clear business focus, concentrating on guided weapons activities;
- elimination of duplicated facilities and excess capacity through rationalisation and consolidation;
- reduction in vertical integration;
- matching Dynamics resources to the needs of the market.

One of the first moves was to instigate a major rationalisation during 1989, closing five of the eight sites and consolidating operations at the three remaining sites: Stevenage, Lostock and Bristol. Manufacturing facilities were centralised at Lostock, design and R&D activities were consolidated at Stevenage, which also contained the business centre, whilst Bristol was to concentrate on software engineering. The rationalisation also represented the first step in an ongoing reduction in the size of the workforce. Between 1988 and the end of 1991, employee numbers were reduced drastically, from 18,700 to 6900. Subsequent downsizing further reduced the size of the workforce, such that by the end of 1995 Dynamics employed around 3000 people.

Key points

- Kawasaki Production System (KPS) was introduced to manufacturing sections in 1990.
- KPS pilot schemes yielded sizeable improvements, including a 50 per cent increase in productivity.

- Continuous Improvement Activity Groups (CIAGs) and Integrated Production Teams were introduced to encourage new teamworking practices.
- In 1992 Engineering for Manufacturing Excellence was introduced to bridge the gap between design engineering and manufacturing.
- In 1994 Design for Product Excellence was introduced to help develop the interface between manufacturing and design as well as helping to create a learning organisation.
- A Concurrent Engineering (CE) initiative was set up, which was driven by change teams to strengthen relationships between the different departments and help to drive CI.

KAWASAKI PRODUCTION SYSTEM (KPS)

At the Lostock site, the consolidation of manufacturing operations had brought together a wide variety of different types of products that had been designed for manufacture at a different site, leading to problems of translation and the need to improve facilities to accommodate the new business. At the same time, in line with the new Dynamics strategy, non-core and non-profitable work needed to be divested and costs, both materials and overheads, had to be drastically reduced. In particular, the direct to indirect employee ratio was far too high. In defining the task that lay ahead, Lostock introduced a manufacturing strategy, consistent with the wider Dynamics business strategy, with the following aims:

- establishment of a Dynamics manufacturing centre at the Lostock site;
- selection and implementation of a new management team;
- planned divestment of non-core and unprofitable work;
- operational focus on assembly, integration and test activities;

☐ in-house manufacturing of key components only, consistent with new aggressive make/buy policy;

☐ overhaul of production scheduling and control systems;

☐ reduction in the cost of production, lead times and inventory levels;

☐ creation of a positive, flexible culture.

Just-in-Time (JIT) and cellular production

In helping to achieve these aims, the company started experimenting with aspects of the JIT approach and introduced the concept of cellular production. Prior to this, the machine shop could be characterised by poor, cramped working conditions, outdated machinery and a bad reputation with customers. The introduction of cellular production was seen as a way of moving over to modern manufacturing techniques. As the operations were reorganised into cells, however, rather than yielding improvements, performance actually deteriorated further.

The reason was simple. Whilst the physical layout elements of JIT had been adopted, there had been little attempt to understand the philosophy and culture of JIT. The combination of cellular layout and traditional control techniques did not allow the generation of the necessary information to facilitate effective production. The situation was further compounded by an attempt to introduce Manufacturing Resource Planning II (MRPII) in 1990 in the hope that this would deal with production control problems, allowing everything else to fall into place.

Eventually it became clear that there was a need to really get to grips with the underlying problems, rather than simply throwing money at them. Looking around at the changes being introduced by 'world class' companies, the enormity of the task that lay ahead became apparent; external help was clearly needed. After much deliberation, Price Waterhouse were chosen to implement the KPS. This was seen as embodying a flexible approach that could be adapted to suit the varying needs of different types of businesses and different size of operations. KPS was based on the concept of JIT, with an emphasis on waste elimination and CI.

To facilitate the change process, a multi-disciplinary team

was formed consisting of both Dynamics personnel and the consultants, the latter being permanent members of the team for a period of about a year. An initial diagnostic review was carried out that revealed the following results:

☐   poor understanding of customer requirements;

☐   very complex process flows;

☐   no control of inventory;

☐   poor response to production problems;

☐   complex lines of responsibility;

☐   low productivity;

☐   negative attitudes.

Implementing change

Implementation started in earnest in 1991 with a pilot on the three production areas of BAe's ALARM line: the machine shop; PCB assembly; and final assembly. Changes introduced included the creation of manufacturing cells, pull scheduling, kanbans*, waste elimination, teamworking and problem solving. Initially, KPS was introduced into each of the production areas separately, but once it became established the production areas were linked together and synchronised.

The pilots proved to be a huge success, yielding sizeable improvements in both tangible and non-tangible performance indicators:

☐   production cycle time reduced by 50 per cent;

☐   batch size reduced by between 50 and 75 per cent;

☐   work in progress reduced by 60 per cent;

☐   productivity increased over 50 per cent;

☐   increased operator satisfaction;

☐   increased operational control and responsiveness.

Consequently, six months down the line, the decision was taken to roll out KPS across all lines. This was implemented gradually over the next three years, since it was felt that a 'big bang'

---

*A communication tool in the Just-in-Time production and inventory control system.

approach to implementation would have proved to be too much of a culture shock. As the implementation progressed, techniques were refined and new elements introduced into the change programme.

Team-building lay at the heart of the changes, which meant undergoing a massive learning process in moving towards new ways of working and learning how to become 'team players'. Two main vehicles were introduced to implement the new team-working practices: Continuous Improvement Action Groups (CIAGs) and Integrated Production Teams.

TEAM-BUILDING

Improvement groups

CIAGS consisted of small groups of employees, mainly operators and engineers, who came together outside their normal work activities to generate specific process improvements, disbanding once the problem had been solved. Typically, teams went off-line for about one hour each week with a facilitator. Although employees had participated in team-building training, the CIAGs were initially launched without training employees in the process and tools of problem-solving. Consequently, the meetings often degenerated into whingeing sessions, since people tended to focus on the problems themselves as they lacked the necessary tools to generate appropriate solutions. Team members also lacked the confidence to take actions themselves, such that corrective actions were predominantly undertaken by the engineers. To rectify these problems, training was introduced as one of the seven basic tools of quality and a group of 12 individuals, who were trained first, became the training team. Having solved some of the initial teething problems, the numbers of CIAGs in operation grew significantly.

Suggestion scheme

The introduction of CIAGs was accompanied by a sharp rise in the number of ideas submitted to the suggestion scheme.

The suggestion scheme was a long-running, traditional-style

scheme that gave people substantial financial rewards on an individual basis. With the introduction of CIAGs, it was found that people were taking ideas away from the meetings and submitting them to the suggestion scheme as individual ideas. In line with the new teamworking philosophy, the scheme was revised so that team suggestions received greater rewards than individual ones.

To reinforce the importance of incremental improvement, the company also started to move away from direct financial rewards to a points-based system. Employees were able to build up points which they could exchange for Capital Bonds, redeemable at a wide range of high street retailers. Annual awards were also introduced for the best suggestion and for best team of the year (ie the team with the highest number of points). The new-style scheme, administered from Lostock but run on a company-wide basis, proved to be highly successful. To ensure that the momentum was maintained, it was relaunched annually with a new publicity drive.

Work-based teams

The Integrated Production Teams were dedicated to supporting production and consisted of small, focused teams based around each manufacturing cell, involving both direct operational staff and support staff. The teams met twice a day. The first meeting was in the morning to discuss production schedules and any problems that had arisen. For each problem, agreement was reached on who 'owned' the problem and what corrective action was to be taken. The second, shorter, meeting was held mid-afternoon to check that everything had gone as planned and to review potential problems for the following day. The teams were left to run the meetings themselves, although facilitators were used if a team was found to be struggling.

While the work-based teams played a key role in problem-solving within the manufacturing cells, the number of improvement teams grew quickly and spread to most areas, including some outside manufacturing (eg purchasing), involving around 90 per cent of the workforce.

SPREADING CI TO SUPPLY CHAINS AND PURCHASING FUNCTIONS

Although the Kawasaki Production System largely focused on the manufacturing operations, the changes encompassed supply chain management and, therefore, spread improvement activity into the purchasing function – the Material Directorate – which was based at Stevenage. Improvement within this area had the potential to make a significant impact on the organisation as a whole, since 80 per cent of components were supplied by sub-contractors.

Material Quality Strategy

Prior to the introduction of a new Material Quality Strategy, supplier performance was characterised by high costs, late delivery and poor quality. As JIT was introduced in the manufacturing operations, the buffer of stocks between the supplier and production was effectively eliminated and the impact of late delivery on projects could no longer be tolerated. Under the Material Quality Strategy, a new system was introduced for selecting the supplier base, and efforts were devoted to moving away from the traditional adversarial relationships. To help develop the appropriate skills for the new-style relationships, increasing emphasis was placed on the development of personnel.

The improvement programme represented a major cultural change and marked a turning point in relationships with suppliers, moving toward a climate of mutual dependence and focusing on improving lead times through the joint elimination of waste in the supply chain. However, by focusing largely on making improvements with the smaller suppliers, over whom Dynamics had more influence, the potential of the programme was not exploited to its full extent. As one manager commented,

We tackled the easy part of the 80 per cent. Probably the 20 per cent of the 80 per cent.

Consequently, progress was fairly limited and improvements were sporadic.

Despite facilitating some change within the Material Directorate, the scope of change was predominantly confined to the Lostock site. As well as transforming the production operations, the introduction of KPS brought about a whole cultural shift at Lostock. This significant change was achieved despite a climate of uncertainty in relation to job security.

The downside, however, was that the cultural barriers between the Lostock and Stevenage sites – and therefore between the manufacturing and design functions – were heightened. If this was to be eliminated, change needed to be pushed all the way through the organisation. A number of successive initiatives proceeded to do this.

Engineering for Manufacturing Excellence

As the introduction of the KPS at Lostock started to establish more effective production methods, the need for improvement activities to move into the areas that interfaced with production, such as design and engineering, was increasingly highlighted. Historically, the functional organisational structure, coupled with the physical distance between the Lostock and Stevenage sites, resulted in little overlap and poor communication between these separate functional areas.

In order to strengthen links and bridge the gap between design, engineering and manufacturing, a new Manufacturing Engineering function was created. Within this function, a Manufacturing System Design department was set up to deliver manufacturing systems into the operations side of the organisation.

As KPS became established, manufacturing started to demand systems to suit the new techniques and systems they had adopted from the Manufacturing Systems Design area. The response was the Engineering for Manufacturing Excellence initiative, introduced in 1992, the prime objective of which was to ensure that new production systems were designed which were complementary to the production methods and techniques that had been adopted at Lostock. Prior to this, manufacturing systems design had been predominantly an *ad hoc* process, whereby the manufacturing systems would be put together by production engineers at Lostock as best they could after the product design had been completed. Under the new approach, the design phase of a project would include both the product design and the manufacturing systems design.

Training

This presented a major challenge and the need to climb a steep learning curve in adopting new approaches to the design of manufacturing systems. To help bring about the necessary learning, the Engineering for Manufacturing Excellence initiative focused on the concept of simultaneous engineering. A team of Dynamics staff worked with consultants, again from Price Waterhouse, to clarify the needs of the department and the content of the programme.

The outcome was the development of a training programme for everyone in the Manufacturing Systems department, plus others who interfaced with the department. In total, around 150 people received the training over a 9–12 month period. Initially the courses were run by Price Waterhouse, although as time progressed the tutoring role was handed over to internal staff. The training incorporated the following modules:

□ introduction to simultaneous engineering;
□ manufacturing strategy for competitive advantage;
□ material systems;
□ manufacturing processes and cell design;
□ product design specification;
□ human resource integration;
□ life-cycle management.

Results

Despite some initial scepticism, people were generally in favour of the change and, according to one manager, the department had a real sense of purpose, a real 'buzz', at the time. The programme had introduced a fairly radical change in the ways of working and had brought about a general acceptance and belief that manufacturing systems actually needed to be designed rather than just thrown together.

The Engineering for Manufacturing Excellence initiative contributed to developing a culture based on involvement and CI as a natural way of working. It also helped to establish more effective communication between the Stevenage and Lostock sites and, therefore, played an important role in bridging the cultural gap between the two. Manufacturing Systems Design staff started working more closely with production staff in problem-solving activities through CIAGs.

Trying to initiate CIAGs within the department itself, however, proved to be less successful, mainly due to work pressures being allowed to take priority over CI activities. The lack of success of formal CI vehicles was, though, partly offset by the developing culture of CI.

DESIGN FOR PRODUCT EXCELLENCE

The introduction of CI into the manufacturing and Manufacturing Systems Design areas had gone some way towards improving the manufacturing–design interface although, as yet, the interface between manufacturing and the actual product design had not been addressed. The changes made to date had, however, created increasing pressures for improving the product design process. The Design for Product Excellence initiative, launched in 1994, aimed to bring about the necessary improvement through two key streams of activity: Business Process Re-engineering, and creating a 'learning organisation'.

Under the Business Process Re-engineering stream of activity, an analysis of the whole design process was undertaken to ascertain how it could best be reconfigured to meet a set of critical success factors. The analysis identified six key areas in design (eg integration of sub-systems, management of sub-contract testing) and for each area a team of ten people was set up to analyse how things were currently done. The outcome was to develop a new model, as the basis of the design process – a generic model that could be applied to any area.

In introducing the concept of a learning organisation, one of the key aims was to try and get people to consider the implications of their activities outside their immediate work area. A number of training modules were developed to support this new mindset: for example, including modules on supply chain management, design for manufacturing and life-cycle costing, etc. The training, delivered by senior managers in the design area, required participants to conduct case studies on aspects of their projects and analyse the impact of their action for other functions. They were required to identify where improvements could be made, with the additional aim of helping to break down barriers.

As with the majority of previous initiatives, and the System Engineering Excellence initiative that followed in 1995, the main barriers experienced related to the functionally-bounded nature of the improvement activities.

CONCURRENT ENGINEERING (CE)

It was recognised that, although previous initiatives had made significant improvements, these had tended to be localised rather than company-wide.

Attempts to drive the improvement out of specific functional areas, and across other parts of the organisation had been less successful. The Concurrent Engineering programme represented an attempt to address this limitation by driving change down from the top of the organisation.

The need for CE was largely born out of problems in the product development cycle, whereby the company was consistently failing to achieve targets in terms of time, cost and the appropriate quality. Using CE, therefore, the aim was to shorten the product development cycle and reduce costs and the time to market. It was felt that the most significant problems lay at the functional interfaces and, whilst previous initiatives had generated improvements within functional areas, they had done little to break down interfunctional barriers.

Change Team

The Change Team was a permanent, multi-disciplinary team of 12 to 18 representatives from different parts of the company.

They were seconded to the team for a fixed period, typically between a year and 18 months, and reported straight into the board of directors. The concept of the Change Team was originally set up by consultants as part of an early project control initiative. It was decided to continue with the vehicle as a way of driving organisational change, and its role evolved into trying to instil CE. To this end, the Change Team's brief was to carry out an analysis of the problem, identify solutions and design and implement changes. More specifically, the team adopted a number of aims:

☐ maintain the process of cultural change and CI;

☐ increase the probability of winning future orders through lower costs, speed to market and improved communications;

☐ improve customer satisfaction and employee satisfaction.

ROLE OF CE IN IMPROVING INTERDEPARTMENTAL RELATIONS

Existing interdepartmental relations could be characterised by an 'over the wall' approach where a department or function carried out its stage of the work consecutively and then passed it 'over the wall' to the next stage, with little interest in the project once their part had been completed. Using CE, the aim was to overlap the individual processes and break down the sequential barriers. This would mean getting people involved much earlier in the design phase, when it would be less costly to make changes. Traditionally, many changes were made much later in the process, when significant time and money had already been invested in development.

Initially, the Change Team spent some time developing a detailed picture of how the design process currently operated, looking at how people did their jobs, the problems they faced and how they interfaced with other departments. They invited people to comment on the results of this analysis and the comments were incorporated into the final analysis.

One of the main findings was that there was a tendency for people to ignore or forget about the target cost. This highlighted the need for mechanisms to reinforce the target cost at all stages in the product introduction process. Another important learning point that emerged from the analysis was the need to include major suppliers in the process, since these had a valuable input as experts in their own field and could help to solve problems and suggest modifications.

Having identified the major problem areas, a series of workshops were run to communicate the concepts of CE to the majority of the workforce, illustrating achievements that other companies had realised. These helped to convince people of the potential benefits of CE. Aside from the educational task of the workshops, the major change that came out of the CE initiative was the introduction of teamworking in the development side of the business. Considerable time and resources were invested in developing and supporting team-working.

Building on the concept of the Integrated Production Teams that had been introduced into manufacturing, a hierarchy of multi-disciplinary development teams were set up for each project sub-level, cutting across the 'walls' between the functional departments. The teams met regularly, perhaps two to three times per week, for short, stand-up meetings with a rotating facilitator and scribe. The meetings were intended primarily as a communication mechanism to talk through issues, actions and problems, rather than actually working on problems.

To support the effective operation of the new teams, intensive training was carried out in teamworking skills, covering interpersonal skills, facilitation skills and problem-solving skills. Team leaders also participated in a separate module on leadership skills. The training took place over several days off-site and involved working in groups on real organisational problems. To reinforce the initial training, each department/work area was issued with a handbook on concurrent engineering, containing problem-solving tools and guidelines for situations in which these might be appropriate, which was intended for use as a reference document. Having instilled teamworking on the ASRAAM[3] project, the training was then rolled out to other projects.

To ensure the necessary commitment and support for the multi-disciplinary development teams, a committee was set up

[3] Advance Short Range Air to Air Missile.

for each project prior to implementation. The committee was involved in the design and implementation of training in their area and were responsible for seeing that the momentum of the activity was sustained. As part of the training participants were required to work on specific problems relating to their project, as selected by the committee, which helped to make the training directly relevant to their work and created a greater sense of ownership.

At the time of writing, the teams were still being rolled out across the organisation and the concept was also being introduced in support areas, such as site facilities. A flexible approach to training evolved so that it was relevant to *all* teams working in these areas. Rather than trying to impose the training on work areas, a demand-led approach was adopted, so that work areas would introduce teamworking because they saw it as something worthwhile, rather than being told that they had to use it.

'FIT FOR THE FUTURE'

In mid-1994, Dynamics introduced a major new strategy, 'Fit for the Future', to bring about radical company-wide change. The strategy consisted of three major strands, which were implemented simultaneously, as illustrated in Figure 1.1.

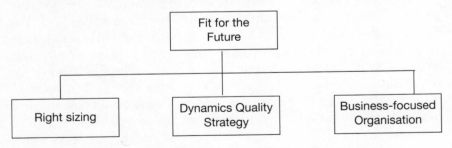

Figure 1.1: *Fit for the Future strategy*

Right sizing

Right sizing involved a further scaling down of the workforce, with approximately 1000 redundancies over a two-year period, to reach an optimum size of around 3000 employees. Reduction in size and, therefore, space enabled significant reduction in the company's cost base.

Business-focused organisation

The creation of a business-focused organisation involved company-wide reorganisation, moving from the previous functional structure to a product/project-driven structure. The functional directorates were replaced by three multi-disciplinary business directorates which cut across the three sites: Air Defence, Air Weapons and Anti-Armour & Naval. One of the key objectives behind the creation of a 'business-focused organisation' was to increase customer orientation by aligning the organisation with its major customers.

The organisation was historically very matrix-dominated: new projects would be carved up into 'packages' and passed on to functional managers. This created a very polarised organisation, where individuals worried about their specific aspect of the project, with little concern about the project as a whole. This created problems for the project management team:

> The project management team had virtually no people leadership requirements at all, yet they were the people who were responsible for delivering the profit, delivering the financial performance and delivering the technical performance.

Under the new structure, functional structures no longer cut across the project as a whole; those managing the project (or sub-project) were also given the responsibility for every aspect of the job and the project team as a whole. The new structure was also intended to promote and reinforce team-working and a more people-focused approach, reflecting the strategic recognition that this is where many of the problems lie.

Consequently, under the new strategy there was a growing emphasis on organising people in ways that gave them greater autonomy, and effecting a corresponding reorientation in the role of management.

Progress

By mid-1995, Dynamics was about a year into the reorganisation with around two-thirds of the workforce having been integrated into the new business directorates. Areas which were still to be integrated into the directorates included sales, customer support, the central procurement role, the old Technology Directorate and some operations and finance. The physical relocation of people under the new directorates was still to be completed and had formed the subject of much debate. The original intention was that people would not be relocated. Against this, however, it was argued that simply redrawing the lines on the organisational chart was unlikely to bring about the desired change; moving people physically together would help to communicate and reinforce the importance of the key changes under the new strategy.

The fact that the company maintained a reasonably profitable business (it has only been out of the black for two of the last eight years) despite the severe downfall in demand suggests that the company faced up to its competitive challenges fairly early on and took drastic steps to respond. Although the size of the workforce reduced considerably after the redundancies, turnover has increased. This reflects both the adoption of more modern capital intensive methods and substantial efficiency improvements.

Road show

Despite the benefits that had been realised through the various improvement programmes, a number of barriers persisted in preventing such improvement efforts from reaching their full potential. In 1994 a road show was organised, bringing together various improvement activities from across the organisation, to highlight their achievements. This revealed that there were over 100 separate improvement programmes which had sprung up across the organisation.

Whilst this indicated a significant level of grass roots activity, each of the programmes ran independently with no overall coordination, and each focused on a specific area within the company. With no clear focus from the top, the various change programmes were not aligned to the strategic imperatives nor locked into real business problems. Resources were also being wasted since there was a significant degree of overlap between individual programmes which were often tackling similar or related issues.

An attitude survey highlighted employee concerns that there were too many stand-alone change programmes – people were suffering from 'initiative fatigue'. This, in particular, supported the need for a more coordinated approach.

Coordinating CI through Dynamics Quality Strategy (DQS)

The 1994 road show was the impetus behind the DQS – a structured company-wide improvement programme to support a more coordinated approach to CI. In March 1995 the DQS was launched through another road show which was taken around all sites. In all, the strategy consisted of 24 programmes. Although each of these was clearly identifiable, the DQS also highlighted their interdependencies.

It is important to note that many of the features of the strategy were not entirely new; what *was* new was the integration of successful activities into one coherent strategic framework. By doing this, the DQS made more effective use of resources by eliminating overlaps and by identifying gaps and deficiencies.

Elements of the DQS

The 24 programmes were further categorised as strategic, tactical or operational:

☐ **ten were classed as strategic programmes** which affected all areas of the business, and impacted on all or most of the critical success factors (eg systems process, success through learning);

☐ **six were classed as tactical programmes** which focused on establishing specific parts of the organisation as 'Areas of Excellence' (eg systems technology programme);

☐ **eight were classed as operational programmes**, focused on very localised improvement activities which required a low level of funding.

Each of the individual programmes was linked to the business aims, and each included a list of measurements to monitor improvements and help justify investments. Sponsoring directors (with overall responsibility for the programme) and improvement leaders were appointed to coordinate activities within individual improvement programmes.

OVERALL STRATEGY REVIEW

A Quality Council was responsible for ongoing review of the effectiveness of the DQS, through an annual diagnostic exercise which included customer, supplier and employee attitude surveys. In particular, assessments against the European Foundation for Quality Management (EFQM) Model for Business Excellence were used to identify where efforts should be made to improve business. This is linked to four key business drivers:

- □ effective and satisfied people;
- □ financial return;
- □ orders at the right price;
- □ customer satisfaction.

OUTCOMES

Despite the significant progress that had been made with improvement efforts, a general reluctance to change persisted within the company, despite the climate of job insecurity. There was a tendency for some people to view change as something that was forced on them and was over and above their job role. To a certain extent these types of attitudes can be attributed to the way that the company has handled change in the past. The continual stream of new initiatives gives rise to sentiments that people have heard it all before. With the 'Fit for the Future' change programme, there were some sentiments that the pace of change was possibly too rapid, with all elements being introduced simultaneously. However, it was still too early in the implementation of the programme to assess its effectiveness and people's reactions to the change.

BAe – REVIEW OF IMPLEMENTATION

Key points

- The approach to change at BAe was business-focused and project-driven, starting with the introduction of new production systems. The focus of improvement then moved out to incorporate different areas within the company, and also some suppliers.

- The change process involved a radical reorganisation of regular work practices. A forward planning approach to change was adopted which involved identifying the areas of the company which could make a significant impact on the organisation as a whole, and getting rid of non-profit core areas.

- Teamwork was at the heart of the improvement process – in particular, developing links between different functions.

- The initiatives have resulted in a radical change in the way of working and brought about the belief that manufacturing systems need to be designed rather than put together in an *ad hoc* fashion.

- Tangible gains include the elimination of duplicated activities and increased productivity. The changes have also contributed to an improvement in cross-boundary working. This has helped to bridge the gaps between different units such as manufacturing, design and engineering as well as improve working relationships across two different sites.

Summary

The BAe case study illustrates some of the advantages associated with adopting a highly structured approach to change. The initiatives have helped to encourage the development of some of the behaviours associated with CI implementation, such as 'high involvement' and effective working across internal and external divisions.

This case demonstrates the role of learning in CI implementation and the successful use of enabling mechanisms to evaluate the impact of the change programmes. For example, feedback from an employee attitude survey highlighted the need for coordination between different initiatives. In response to this information the company has adopted a more effective system of project management, which prioritises and categorises activities into strategic, functional or small-scale initiatives.

One of the learning points from this case is how BAe went about developing an organisation which was both business-focused and 'people-centred'. The emphasis was on organising people in a way which gave them greater autonomy and improved teamwork and communication. By moving people physically together, rather than just redrawing lines on the organisational chart, and by coordinating the various improvement activities, the company has helped to promote the desired change.

Case 2
NPI – CARDIFF

NPI[4] is one of the largest mutual companies in the UK. Established over 150 years ago, it specialises in pensions and retirement-related products and employs over 1500 people. The Cardiff office, which is the focus for this case study, was set up in 1989 and is responsible for group and company pension schemes.

OVERVIEW OF CASE

This case will focus mainly on events at NPI's operations in Cardiff. Following a recognition of the need for enhanced customer services, the Life Manager introduced a Total Quality Management training package during 1988 and 1989. The initiative applied to the Customer Service Division, based in Cardiff.

However, it soon became apparent that many of the problems experienced by the Customer Service Division were due to poor communication and interaction between the various departments across the company. It was decided that the way forward was to introduce a company-wide policy of improvement (Quality Improvement Process).

In 1989, a company-wide Quality Improvement Team was set up which was chaired by the Quality Manager, John Morgan and, two years later, by the Chief Executive.

---

[4] Formerly known as National Provident Institution.

The Quality Improvement Strategy evolved in two phases over the next few years. In the first instance activities focused on aligning processes and systems to the overall business aims, while the second phase focused on improving customer satisfaction through quality, (eg through one-to-one contact with clients, better customer service and increased staff morale). Staff were given formal training and new modes of measurement were introduced to help bring about the desired change. The Quality Improvement Programme has made substantial progress in initiating cultural change and making quality improvement integral to everyday work.

BACKGROUND

Within the UK, NPI is one of the largest mutual life and insurance companies,[5] with an annual turnover in excess of £1 billion. It manages investments of around £9 billion on behalf of more than 500,000 members. The company specialises in providing pensions and other retirement-related products.

NPI employs approximately 1500 employees, the majority of whom work at Tunbridge Wells, where the Head Office is based. A further 300 people are employed at Cardiff and there are also 80 investment staff located in London. The success of the company in the application of quality and CI principles is reflected in a number of awards, as are outlined below.

☐ Pension Transfer Plan product (at Cardiff) was BS5750 accredited (August 1994).

☐ Most Improved Life Office Award – Financial Adviser Service Awards (1993) and gained the inaugural Wales Quality Award in autumn 1994 for customer satisfaction.

☐ Institute of Administrative Management Quality Award in June 1994, 'Achieving Total Quality for Success' for NPI as a whole.

☐ In 1995 NPI was the first life assurance company to host the DTI 'Inside UK Enterprise' Scheme and also in 1995 NPI

---

[5] It has no shareholders and all profits are shared out amongst policy-holders.

Cardiff won the Wales Quality Award for Medium Size Businesses.

☐ In 1996 NPI won the Wales Quality Category Service Sector Award, and was one of three finalists out of 200 entrants for the Meridian Business Excellence Award.

HISTORY

By the 1980s, NPI had evolved a divisional structure, with each division representing a specific functional area covering Finance, Assets, Information Systems, Human Resources, Marketing and Sales and Customer Service.

NPI Cardiff was established in 1989 when the company decided to split the Customer Service Division into two separate divisions, one dealing with individual pensions and the other with responsibility for company pensions business.

The company purchased and extensively refurbished the old headquarters of South Glamorgan County Council and the first teams were set up in Cardiff in March 1989. The remainder of the company pensions business had been transferred by the end of 1990.

Operations at Cardiff were divided into two main product areas: group pensions, which administered company-wide pension schemes; and executive pensions, which dealt with pension arrangements for senior-level staff, such as directors, senior managers and owners.[6] Over the last few years the group has developed into a strategic business unit (with its own board and chief executive).

Within each of the product sectors, operational staff were organised into work teams and supervised by an Operations Controller. The Operations Controllers reported to an Operations Manager, who in turn reported to either the Group or Executive Pension Manager, depending on the type of scheme for which they were responsible. Staff in each product area were supported by a Customer Liaison Unit within the customer support areas (Figure 2.1).

---

[6] Pension Transfer Plans, which involve a single premium, were also managed within the Executive Pensions area.

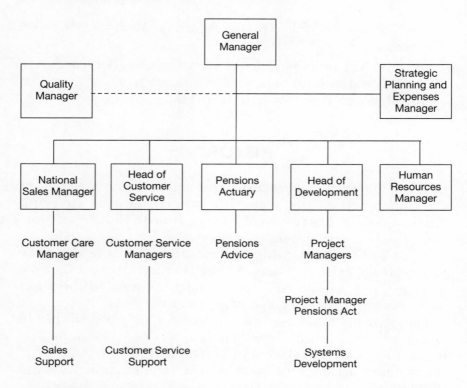

Figure 2.1: *Organisational structure – NPI Group Pensions*

These were set up to manage more substantial enquiries or complaints that could not be dealt with within the teams, although they worked with the teams in solving the problems and improving processes. Staff within these units also carried out small project work and other non-standard activities. To ensure that staff within the Customer Liaison Units did not become too detached from the operational teams, staff were encouraged to move between the two areas.

QUALITY IMPROVEMENT PROCESS (QIP)

Key points

- Problems experienced in the Customer Services Division in the 1980s.

- Company-wide Quality Improvement Process introduced in 1989, which was supported by top management.

- In 1990 the Quality Training programme was delivered to all staff. To ensure that the programme was linked to company objectives, rather than perceived as a training department initiative, the training was delivered by 12 members of middle management.

- The quality message was reinforced through communication mediums such as a newsletter and various team briefings.

Problems

Throughout the 1980s, increasing problems were being experienced within the Customer Service Division and the development of new computer systems to support the administration of new products did not live up to expectations, thus contributing to a major backlog of work. The existing problems were exacerbated by a 10 per cent take up on a direct mail offer in 1985 marking the company's 150th anniversary, which merely added to the backlog. The initial response to address the backlog was simply to bring in more people.

By 1988, John Morgan (Life Manager at the time) had convinced other Customer Service managers of the need to tackle these problems head on. After spending some time researching possible approaches, he put together a Total Quality Management training package for the division. The process of rolling out the training began in 1989 with workshops for managers and supervisors. However, it soon became apparent that most of the problems that were being experienced within the division could not be attributed to customer service alone, but could be traced to the communications and interactions between Customer Service and other divisions. Although the customer service training continued with sessions for operational staff, Morgan and his Customer Service Division colleagues started lobbying NPI senior managers on the need for a company-wide approach to quality improvement.

Senior management support

At first the senior managers were not convinced, maintaining that other divisions were functioning well and it was up to Customer Service to 'get its act together'.

Attitudes at senior management level started to shift, however, after the arrival of a new Human Resources Director, Terry Mullins, who strongly supported the need for a company-wide quality improvement process and had been involved in the implementation of a similar quality initiative in his previous job. Gradually, other members of the senior management team were won over and in mid-1989 gave the go-ahead for taking the Crosby approach to quality company-wide, under the title of the QIP.

This commitment was further reinforced after the senior management team attended a two-day training course on the Quality Improvement Process. As a result, senior management became more actively involved and showed their commitment by opening and attending workshops and Quality Improvement Teams (QITs) training.

Staff training

1990 was predominantly spent developing and delivering education and training courses to all staff. The senior management team released 12 respected middle managers to facilitate the management training sessions in the 'Quality Education System'. In taking this approach, the aim was to ensure that the quality programme was treated as a core business programme rather than a training department initiative. Following the completion of the management training in June 1990, the Crosby training was developed into a customised course for all employees, called Quality Team Education. This training was delivered by managers and supervisors to their work teams over six two-hour sessions (12 hours for all employees). This initial training was completed by the end of December 1990. The fact that the training was delivered by *management* rather than HR helped to increase the profile of the initiative and to gain support from staff.

To ensure that new employees would also receive training in the quality improvement principles, a computer-based training package, 'Second to None', was subsequently developed in-house. This consisted of five modules, each lasting around one hour, supported by a self-learning manual containing exercises and assignments. This package has since been replaced with material that reflects NPI's evolution away from 'pure Crosby'.

QIP teams

One of the first moves in taking the QIP company-wide was to set up a series of QITs.[7] The Chief Executive initially chaired the Steering Committee, which comprised the senior management team.

The corporate Quality Improvement Team was initially chaired by John Morgan and from 1992 by the Chief Executive. Each representative on the corporate QIT then chaired a team at divisional level.

COMMUNICATION

The quality message was reinforced and progress updated by integrating quality into the existing communication system; an effective cascade of meetings and briefing systems. The main elements of this system were:

□   Senior management (company-wide) met weekly to review key operational and business issues. Followed by sessions to brief all staff by the end of the next working day.

□   The outcome of monthly NPI board meetings is briefed to all managers within 24 hours.

[7] Philip Crosby & Associates training materials were used to assist with the implementation.

☐   Biannual half-day briefing sessions for all management on company results and future challenges. Managers then used the material to brief their staff. Operations Controllers met as a group with their Operations Manager on a weekly basis.

☐   Annual briefings, sometimes including videos, to all staff from NPI senior management.

☐   Staff representatives met monthly with managers as a Joint Consultative Committee to discuss any issues raised by staff.

New written communications were also introduced to support the Quality Improvement Process, including a company-wide Quality Update newsletter and Cardiff's own 'Helo!' (*sic*) newsletter, in addition to posters, booklets for all staff and notice-boards. More recently, e-mail has been extensively used.

Stimulating improvement activity (Cardiff)

Key points

- In 1991, a report was developed which measured performance and output against eight key business processes.

- Staff were encouraged to constantly monitor and make improvements to their work processes.

- Statistical Process Control (SPC) was introduced, as well as new measurements on customer satisfaction and error rates.

- A formal recognition system was introduced.

Under the Quality Improvement Process, people were encouraged for the first time to see their administrative procedures in terms of processes. To support the new process orientation, an analysis was conducted to identify key business processes and the current bottlenecks and critical points for each. A project team of management information staff, aided by an external consultant, was set up to design a reporting system that would help staff control their daily work processes and generate management information for decision-making. The resulting Process and Performance Analysis (PAPA) identified eight main processes (eg renewals, claims, cash processing) and weekly PAPA reports were introduced in 1991, summarising data on key performance criteria, work throughput and productivity.

Later, in 1992, all main processes were written up in the 'Bible of Processes', providing a central record of the strengths and weaknesses, effectiveness and efficiency of each main process. Members of the management team were appointed as Process Owners, to ensure that entries in the 'Bible' were maintained.

Although no formal improvement vehicles were introduced, people were encouraged to make improvement suggestions and follow them through. Objectives for individuals and teams included:

- identify your processes;
- identify your customers and suppliers and talk to them;
- review the processes;
- ensure that requirements are understood and agreed;
- put measurements into place to assess performance;
- identify and act on improvement opportunities.

However, it soon became apparent that not all staff were taking the time out to identify improvement opportunities. People argued that work pressures made it difficult to set aside the time, particularly those whose work performance was judged against time-based criteria. Consequently, 'Quality Time' was introduced, whereby all work groups were encouraged to designate a weekly time slot for reviewing processes and identifying ways to improve quality. This proved successful in the early stages of the programme. Later on, as people became more familiar with identifying opportunities for improvement, there was less need for a formalised time slot. Instead people tended to meet and raise issues as and when required.

Ideas for improvements could be dealt with in a number of ways. Typically, an individual would approach their Operations Controller with an idea which, if appropriate, would be put to the rest of the work team for discussion. Minor changes that did not affect other work groups could be introduced immediately by the work team. Suggestions for process changes were dealt with more formally, either by the Customer Liaison Units for more minor changes, or by a project team within Management Services (now Divisional Projects) for more substantial changes.

System changes were dealt with by raising a Systems Query Report (SQR). This formal process ensured that change was consistent across all areas that were affected. The SQR forms were usually completed by supervisory staff, so an individual or team would need to convince them of the need for change. Although the SQR predated the quality improvement process, the forms were updated to include a measure of the Price Of Non-Conformance (PONC) to help determine priorities.

Introducing monitoring and measuring systems

Several exercises were conducted in calculating a company-wide PONC, to help to identify some of the main problem areas and raise awareness of the potential for improvement. One of these indicated a PONC of about 18 per cent across the company. An emphasis on measurement was enhanced by the introduction of new performance measures for error rates and customer satisfaction and the introduction of Statistical Process Control (SPC). SPC training was introduced following the original quality training, to help the work teams monitor and improve their processes. To stress the importance of measurement, several 'measurement days' were run, where senior managers visited operations teams to help them review their measurement activity and understand their barriers to quality improvement.

Use of measurement in focusing improvement activities

The introduction of customer satisfaction measures, such as compliments and complaints, helped to focus people to take action. A junior clerk in Cardiff noted that there were a number of customer complaints relating to one particular procedure. The procedure which was causing problems involved insurance companies having to get authority from the Inland Revenue to issue customer refunds on premiums under £1000. This was time-consuming and laborious and did not meet customer requirements.

As a result the employee suggested that insurance companies

should be able to give refunds under £1000 directly to the customer, without involving the Inland Revenue in the process. The initiative taken at NPI Cardiff has resulted in a change in the process for the industry as a whole.

RECOGNITION SYSTEM

To encourage employees to participate in improvement activities, a formal recognition award scheme was introduced: the Quality Qube (a paperweight). The Qube was awarded monthly by the Cardiff QIT, as in all other divisions.

In addition to the Qube, the recipient was also awarded a certificate and a personal reward of his/her choice, such as a restaurant voucher or theatre tickets. Other achievements which did not win the Qube but were deemed worthy of recognition were also publicised. Every quarter the Cardiff QIT nominated one person or team for the corporate Quality Qube. Winners were publicised through posters and communications in the 'Quality Update' bulletins.

Managers were also encouraged to recognise their employees' efforts informally, either through a verbal thank you or through small gifts. One manager, for example, bought bottles of wine for his staff in recognition of their efforts in significantly raising customer satisfaction levels.

Enhancing recognition

Although it was a formal recognition system, the Quality Qube proved to be a fairly narrow system, with wider, more informal recognition left to the discretion of individual managers. Consequently levels of and approaches to informal recognition tended to vary from manager to manager. Some employees felt that recognition was more forthcoming for improvement activity within formal project work than for improvements that arose from normal teamwork.

In the latter case, the acknowledgement is unlikely to extend any further than the immediate supervisor. As one employee stated:

If you don't blow your own trumpet you won't get any recognition unless it is obvious.

To try to overcome this problem and stimulate wider recognition, a Recognition Register was introduced in 1994. This was displayed in the staff restaurant and recorded details of customer compliments and the photographs of the staff who received them. Visitors were encouraged to look at it. Further, in 1995, a 'thank you' template was introduced on the e-mail system to encourage managers to recognise their staff.

QIP questionnaire

In January 1996 a staff survey was carried out. One of the key issues which emerged was that employees felt the recognition system did not effectively capture their improvement efforts. While the results showed that 73 per cent felt empowered (compared to 47 per cent in 1995), it still left 400 people who did not feel empowered.

In April 1996, NPI had the novel idea of getting managers to walk around their departments with a sandwich board, on which people were encouraged to paste suggestions about how to improve empowerment and recognition in the company.

New recognition scheme

As a result a new recognition scheme was launched; QIT teams were given new recognition cheque-books and points for improvements could be turned into prizes. The points were awarded on an individual basis and anyone could nominate anyone else. To encourage recognition, people making nominations received one point. Each nominee secured five points, with quarterly winner(s) receiving an additional ten points. The nominations were handed into the local QITs (who held the cheque-books) and prizes were awarded accordingly, from five point prizes (worth approximately £5) to 100 point prizes, which included a compact disc player, a weekend break and £100 vouchers.

There are certain categories and criteria to be met before a prize can be awarded. Usually, a member of the QIT team will go out and talk to the person who has been nominated, and make sure the criteria are fulfilled. Winners of improvement awards are invited to a special recognition meeting/buffet (which is attended by all senior management and a selection of managers, as well as previous winners) and are given certificates. This new initiative has helped to bring about a renewed enthusiasm and generate more interest in CI. A 1997 survey report shows that 83 per cent of people now feel empowered, and that 75 per cent think recognition has improved in the last 12 months:

> If I want to change something I can put my idea forward and get it done, we have good communication with the customer and management have realised this and provided money to support improvement and change.[8]

Strategy development

> ### Key points
>
> - Movement away from Crosby approach and greater links made between Quality Improvement Process and overall strategy.
> - Transition from improving the quality of general processes and procedures to increasing customer satisfaction.
> - 'Operation Satisfied Customer' – focused on clearing up work backlogs so that staff could concentrate on their main priority, the external customer.
> - The CI strategy model was developed which identified three distinct market segments, each with their own marketing strategy.
> - Staff were given training to enhance communication with customers (Cardiff Customer Focus).
> - Staff were given responsibility for dealing with individual portfolios of schemes which helped to create stronger relationships between the company and its customers.

[8] Quote from one of the employees from Cardiff on an internal NPI video on quality.

For the original company-wide launch of the Quality Improvement Process a specific quality plan, based on the 14 Crosby steps, was developed to guide the introduction across the whole of the organisation. Although this proved useful in initiating widespread involvement in quality improvement, by the end of 1991 it was decided to move away from the Crosby approach. The main concern was that it had introduced a whole range of parallel organisational structures and systems. As Morgan, the Quality Manager commented:

> We had allowed it to become very messy, very bureaucratic. It was an entirely additional organisation. Despite that we actually made some reasonable progress.

It was felt that improvement activities would be more effective if integrated into normal organisational structures and processes. Consequently, all the separate quality 'machinery', with the exception of the QITs, was disbanded. To demonstrate the integral nature of quality improvement, the business plans were rewritten so that the objectives were clearly expressed in terms of the 'quality language' (customer requirements, process orientation, etc).

'OPERATION SATISFIED CUSTOMER'

The new objectives also placed an increasing emphasis on customer needs and requirements. Whilst the Crosby approach had introduced the concept of customer focus, in practice this had often translated into an over-emphasis on the internal, as opposed to external, customer. Therefore, although a lot of work had been carried out in reducing the PONC, this had not always been to the advantage of the external customer.

The Cardiff QIT promoted a customer orientation through the 'Operation Satisfied Customer' initiative over 1991 and 1992 (parts one and two). This was supported in 1992 by Task A1, set up to investigate how to clear the work backlogs. Although Task A1 was carried out by Cardiff personnel, it was designated a 'corporate level key task' because the Head Office recognised that service levels at Cardiff were having an adverse effect on the business as a whole. Additional corporate resources and support were made available.

Building on the progress made by Operation Satisfied Customer I and Task A1, the second phase of Operation Satisfied Customer was able to move away from the crisis-driven approach of the first phase (ie clearing the backlogs), towards an emphasis on delivering customer requirements. Market orientation courses were introduced to help develop a better understanding of customer satisfaction. From 1993 onwards the approach became increasingly proactive, with the development of a strategy and vision for Cardiff based on the principles of quality and CI (see Figure 2.2).

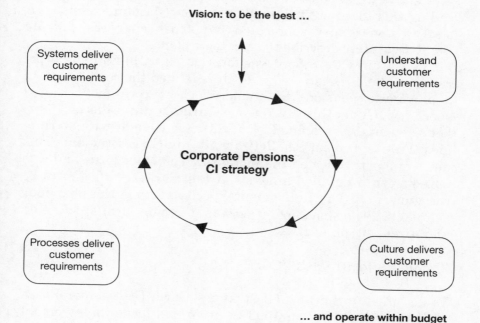

Figure 2.2: *CI strategy model*

This highlighted a transformation process for the organisation, moving from a defensive phase of avoiding doing what the customers did not like, through a transitional phase of identifying customer requirements, to an assertive phase which involves meeting these customer requirements and continually reviewing and improving. In 1994 the Group Transfer Scheme was developed by NPI. This was a facility for customers to transfer to another company, free of charge or penalty, if they were unhappy with any aspect of service provision at NPI. This was a brave step for the company to take, but so far no one has taken up the offer, which is a positive reflection on the group.

This represented the first evolution of a CI strategy, initially focusing on improving procedures to increase customer satisfaction, but later broadening to encompass the whole system. In helping senior managers to develop the CI strategy model, they were trained in the seven management and planning tools.[9] The new strategy was communicated by involving managers in interactive workshops. Managers were then responsible for cascading this to all staff through a series of briefing sessions. A staff awareness survey indicated that 90 per cent of respondents could accurately describe the strategic plans.

The Cardiff CI strategy was formulated within a new corporate level business strategy, which redefined the company from a 'provider of pensions' to the more focused 'retirement-related specialist'. Under this new business strategy, three distinct market segments were defined, each with its own marketing strategies: 'Pre-Retirement'; 'At Retirement'; and 'In Retirement'. This new emphasis reflected the increasing customer focus and was based upon a detailed analysis of the market. NPI aim to be recognised as 'The Retirement Specialist' over the next four years. In 1994 a small operation was set up in Cardiff to develop 'in retirement' products.

'Cardiff Customer Focus' (CCF)

To accompany the new CI strategy, Cardiff Customer Focus (CCF) was launched in 1993 to drive and focus improvement efforts on communicating with the customers. In particular, the initiative aimed to reinforce the personal element of customer contact, for example, through the quality of letters, policy documents and telephone calls. The need to improve the quality of customer contact had been highlighted by research which indicated that this was a major cause of customer dissatisfaction. For example, although customers preferred to deal directly with staff over the phone, many staff felt uncomfortable communicating in this way.

[9] Project staff were also trained in the seven quality tools.

A CCF manager was appointed to coordinate the quality activities and report on progress to the Cardiff QIT. CCF was communicated to employees through briefings from line managers who had specially prepared launch packs. New training programmes were set up for staff in telephone technique and plain English in letter writing and accompanied by a number of control procedures. For example, software was installed to check documents and letters for plain English, and letters and documents were sampled using SPC and the results reported to management weekly.

CCF was the last specific initiative; in the following year the QIT decided that, as CI and customer focus had been integrated into the strategy, there was no need for a specific initiative for 1994.

Development of new customer care skills

The strategic customer orientation was reinforced by changes to the organisational structure. From 1993, NPI Cardiff started moving away from a functional structure, where different teams were responsible for specific aspects of a scheme (eg new business, renewals, claims), towards a 'cellular' product-based structure. Under this new Account Management Strategy, staff were given individual portfolios of schemes to administer on a 'cradle-to-grave' basis. As well as helping to build and strengthen relationships with the customer, the new approach aimed to create a greater sense of ownership and satisfaction amongst employees who would be able to see through any new business from start to finish and have greater control over their work. Scheme administrators were also able to visit their customers – previously the prerogative of managers and sales staff. Staff surveys indicated that staff responded positively to these changes.

The development of the 'cradle-to-grave' approach created new skill requirements. To support this, skill grids were introduced for each employee, indicating each process skill and the level which the individual had attained.

Annual performance and development reviews provided a mechanism for reviewing an individual's performance in relation to key skills and set targets for the following year. From this, training and development needs would be discussed and

formulated within a Personal Development Plan. The budget
made provisions for ten days training per person per year.

Measurement of Key Performance Criteria (KPC)

The new strategy at Cardiff was accompanied by mechanisms
to continually review and update the strategy. All of the Cardiff
senior management team were involved in half-year and end-
of-year reviews to evaluate the actual performance against
strategic plans. Performance was evaluated against a number
of Critical Success Factors. These Critical Success Factors
were based on marketing differentiation ambitions, and all
potential developments were evaluated and prioritised against
them.

KEY PERFORMANCE CRITERIA (KPC)

To facilitate the measurement of progress, six KPC were
defined:

1. In line with the strategic focus, customer satisfaction was
   viewed as the most important factor and measured in a number of ways:
   - **IFT Survey**: a twice-yearly survey of Independent Finan-
     cial Advisers carried out by an independent research
     agency. Based on one-hour interviews with 500 IFAs com-
     paring the performance of around 20 companies. The
     results of the IFT survey are used to conduct more detailed
     investigation and help understand exactly what aspects of
     the service cause dissatisfaction ratings;
   - **Gordon Simmons Research survey**: a biannual survey
     also carried out by an independent research agency;
   - in 1993 **The Corporate Monitor** introduced specific
     research relating to the company pensions market, focusing
     on the behaviour and needs of Independent Financial
     Advisers for whom company pensions represents at least 25
     per cent of their income;
   - published surveys, particularly the **Financial Adviser
     Service Awards** – 'Five Star Survey'. This surveys readers

of the magazine to give an independent ranking of companies in the industry.
2. Percentage of work processed in the agreed time standards.
3. Age profile of work in-house.
4. Total hours of work in-house.
5. Age profile of cash being processed.
6. Levels of rework.

Data on KPCs was produced weekly using SPC charts. This was monitored and reviewed by operations controllers and their operations manager on a weekly basis. Every month performance against plans was reviewed by the senior management team. Progress was communicated to employees through weekly feedback, formal half-year and end-of-year feedback, and through the wide circulation of the management reports.

RESULTS

☐ Savings generated through the QIP are estimated to be in the region of £7 million per annum.

☐ In 1993 the company won the Financial Adviser Service Award as the most improved office.

☐ In 1995 results from the Customer Satisfaction Report show that Independent Financial Adviser satisfaction has risen to 70 per cent as compared to 45 per cent in 1992.

☐ Results in December 1996 showed that policy-holder customer satisfaction had increased to 96 per cent.

REVIEWING OVERALL SUCCESS OF CI TO DATE

Over the years the quality improvement programme has made substantial progress in initiating cultural change and making quality improvement integral. The programme was successful in creating a good understanding of CI and its implications at the operational level and attitudes to improvement were largely positive. Internal climate surveys demonstrated that staff recognised the QIP was a catalyst for change rather than a project in itself.

In particular, a culture had been developed where people were open to change and had come to expect it as the norm. As one employee commented:

> People are very receptive to picking up ideas and changing the process. Nobody in Cardiff expects our processes to be the same this time next year.

Under the Quality Improvement Process some progress had been made in improving employee-management relations, particularly between operational staff and operations managers. People felt that the relationships had generally become more open and as a consequence they felt more valued:

> There is still a certain amount of thinking, 'You don't need to know this, this is my job', but this is getting less and is in the specialised areas.

BARRIERS TO IMPROVEMENT

However, there was still a feeling that, as a whole, managerial commitment was patchy and some managers only paid lip service to the Quality Improvement Process. Some employees felt that this lack of commitment was demonstrated by the minimal time they were allowed to spend on improvement activities. Senior managers, in particular, were still seen as more distant:

> Senior management are a bit aloof, even the ones based in Cardiff. You see them walking around but they don't stop to talk to you. It's still a case of 'managers are coming down, let's have a tidy up'.

Further frustrations arose in relation to a perceived lack of action on suggestions. Although ideas which only affected the immediate work team could be implemented easily in the local area, many improvements had wider implications and therefore had to be approved at higher levels. People felt there was often little feedback on ideas which were passed higher. Whether or not feedback was received was seen as being down to the individual manager. This tended to have a discouraging effect and limited feelings of empowerment:

> In the end people felt it wasn't worth coming out with suggestions because nothing would be done about them.

Particular problems were raised with the Systems Query Report system. SQR changes involved filling in a fairly detailed form and calculating the potential cost savings. People found this time-consuming, which discouraged them from putting forward the suggestion in the first place. The SQR would then be prioritised centrally and a 'top ten' produced. Some employees felt that an SQR tended to go to the bottom of the pile unless driven by management.

> You could suggest an improvement that will really improve your work, but because it doesn't affect many people the cost justification isn't high and therefore they won't even consider yours, there'll always be ones higher up. Some SQRs are very old.

FURTHER INITIATIVES IN DEVELOPING A CI CULTURE

Improving levels of empowerment and management commitment were seen as key to the strategic transformation process, in helping the organisation to develop a CI culture. Members of the QIT visited other organisations to identify the characteristics of a CI culture. The seven management and planning tools were then used to group the characteristics and prioritise what actions were needed to develop these characteristics within NPI Cardiff. It was decided that the most pressing issue was to promote empowerment, with a corresponding shift in the role of managers toward leaders and coaches. Two main changes were introduced.

First, an attitude survey was designed and sent out to all staff to ascertain their perceptions of how effectively managers currently lead and coach. The results of the survey will then be used to develop a new 'people satisfaction' Key Performance Criteria, with the survey being repeated annually. Secondly, empowerment workshops were introduced for both managers and work teams. Following the workshops, facilitators help the work teams to complete a self-assessment exercise (entitled 'How empowered is your team?'), covering the following areas:

□   morale;
□   decision-making and control;
□   participation and involvement;
□   cooperation, teamwork and support;
□   communication and feedback;
□   creativity and innovation;
□   role of managers in the organisation;
□   customer satisfaction;
□   recognition;
□   organisational structure.

From this exercise, the team agreed areas most in need of improvement and developed an action plan. The facilitators continue to liaise with the teams in monitoring progress and help them to identify the next priority for improvement by repeating the exercise in, say, six months.

Managers attend separate workshop sessions, with the same material but a different self-assessment exercise in which they evaluate their own performance and develop a personal action plan. Together the managers then develop and agree several improvement actions that they will undertake as a peer group, and publicise these. Progress will be monitored by working in pairs to compare personal action plans and satisfy one another that they address the peer group actions.

At the time of writing it appeared that the initiative has had some impact at NPI in Tunbridge Wells, but has yet to take off with any vigour at Cardiff.

Reinforcing the problem-solving process

The original Crosby training incorporated a formal problem-solving cycle and supporting tools. However, since NPI took a more informal approach to stimulating improvement activity, there were no formal mechanisms for reinforcing the process or ensuring that people always followed it. Although the more informal approach was successful in making improvement integral to employee's normal working activities, a number of drawbacks emerged.

First, without the reinforcement provided by a formal improvement vehicle, much of the training did not take root. Although most people still had the original training manual few, apart from specialist project staff, used it to guide their improvement activities. Secondly, there were no formal procedures to guide employees in raising ideas which could not be dealt with within the work team. Consequently, as highlighted earlier, people often received little feedback and some ideas seemed to get lost in the process.

Journey to Improvement

To help overcome some of these problems, the Journey to Improvement materials were introduced in 1995. This represented an attempt to bring more coherence to the improvement activity by providing a common framework for problem-solving and process improvement activity. The materials consisted of a work-book outlining a Process Improvement and Problem Solving Process and a tool-kit book, to explain which tools were appropriate for particular situations. Six facilitators were trained to support work groups in using the Journey to Improvement material.

It was decided that an effective way of encouraging people to use the materials was by linking it to the Statistical Process Control training. SPC training was originally introduced following the initial Crosby quality training, albeit in a limited form. As SPC has continued to be seen as an important tool for monitoring performance and identifying improvement opportunities, an increasing number of staff have been trained (at least one in each work group).

The Journey to Improvement workshops, lasting one to two hours will be run as a forerunner to the SPC training. Participants will be encouraged to use the Journey to Improvement materials to support the task they will be set in the course of the

SPC workshop. The materials will then provide a framework to resolve problems as the work team continues to use SPC.

Results from recognition meeting (1996)

In February 1996 the second special meeting for recognition of QITs was held and each team provided a brief presentation of their successes, some of which are illustrated below.

☐ 'Same Day Dealings': one group piloted a new approach to dealing with incoming correspondence which has led to real improvements in customer satisfaction, cycle time and productivity, with more than 1000 replies per week to customers on the same day of receipt.

☐ Rates and measures: another group introduced a work control system that has helped remove service backlogs and reduce the production time for special illustrations.

NPI – REVIEW OF IMPLEMENTATION

Key points

■ This case illustrates how CI can be adopted in an office environment. The approach taken was well planned and involved transforming the culture by changing current job roles.

■ The company adopted a phased approach to change, first as a reaction to internal problems, and subsequently as a means of enhancing customer satisfaction.

■ At the heart of the implementation was a need to adopt a process approach to change and to increase customer satisfaction. By identifying and eliminating bottlenecks the company was able to improve internal processes and communication.

■ As a result the changes became an integral part of daily work rather than being seen as an 'add on' to existing procedures. Benefits also include enhanced employee skill levels and increased customer satisfaction.

Summary

The NPI case illustrates how CI can be implemented to ensure high levels of involvement and strategically-aligned activity. Changes in job roles and employee levels of responsibility were central to the programme. This has enabled staff to make a valuable contribution to the change process.

The case demonstrates the importance of leadership, which is one of the behaviours associated with successful implementation. At NPI management played a key role by showing visible commitment to change illustrated by the role of middle management in the delivery of training. Support and resources from Head Office enabled the Customer Service Division to clear up administrative backlogs and focus improvement activities on increasing customer satisfaction.

One of the key examples of good practice in this case is the way in which the company 'managed the gap' between internal and strategic objectives. This was achieved by identifying the key business processes and the skills needed to support them. The use of moving targets and regular assessment has helped sustain the momentum and align CI with the company goals.

Case 3
FORTES BAKERY LIMITED

Fortes Bakery Limited is a medium-sized family-run business which specialises in the wholesale supply of bakery products to the airline industry, with customers based at Gatwick, Heathrow, Stansted and Luton airports and other caterers nationwide. The company has approximately 80 employees.

OVERVIEW OF CASE

Over the last five years Fortes has undergone a number of changes which have helped them to become world-class suppliers to their customers. In 1991 the company moved exclusively into supplying the airline catering industry and they have achieved competitive advantage through the systematic application of quality and standards to all procedures. The move was an attractive proposition for Fortes, as the demand for variety in airline catering was matched by the diversity in Fortes' product range. The company needed, however, to undergo a number of changes and improvements in order to capitalise on this niche market.

Changes in legislation and standards meant that the food industry had to implement more stringent health and safety and hygiene regulations. With the introduction of Total Quality Management (TQM) and Investors In People (IIP) the company has helped to bring about a cultural change which encourages teamworking and training at all levels. The management at Fortes have undergone a learning process over the last few years which has resulted in a very 'hands on' approach to management and a commitment to leading by example. The company identifies CI as being closely linked to quality and effective teamworking, and CI activities concentrate on promoting these values. Fortes' milestones along the CI journey can be broadly outlined by the following objectives and achievements.

Key points

- To introduce a formal set of procedures which can be measured and evaluated to ensure best practice. This is being achieved through the introduction of ISO9002.

- To train the Senior Management Team in leadership and facilitator skills.

- To train and develop staff to understand and share a common approach to quality. This is being achieved through Total Quality Management.[10]

- To develop a culture that supports and encourages teamworking. This is being achieved through the establishment of problem-solving teams called Quality Improvement Process teams (QIPs).

- To encourage learning, training and multi-skilling through IIP and NVQs.

BACKGROUND

Founded in 1932 by the grandfather of the current directors, the business was a traditional craft bakery which had a number of cafés and bakeries in the Hove and Brighton area of East Sussex. The 1960s and 1970s represented a period of growth for Fortes, when products were in demand and the company was profitable. In the late 1980s the company recruited a new Sales

[10] Called Total Quality (TQ) at Fortes.

and Marketing Director, who highlighted the benefits associated with concentrating solely on the airlines market.

The in-flight catering industry had not been saturated with suppliers and Fortes, with their track record of providing quality services, saw a gap in the market where they could achieve competitive advantage. In 1989 the company moved to a site in nearby Burgess Hill in West Sussex, which was more modern and more appropriate for food production.

CHANGING COMPETITIVE ENVIRONMENT

In the late 1980s and early 1990s the company began to experience pressure due to external crises such as the recession and the Gulf War which drastically hit the airline industry. Competition and price pressures became severe and led to a decline in profitability and serious cash flow problems. The company could not afford to cut costs in raw materials as this would affect the quality of the finished product, and perhaps lose customers who had come to expect a particular high standard.

At this time airline catering was going through enforced changes in hygiene standards due to new regulations. This included the introduction of protective clothing. Fortes naturally followed suit, which helped them to develop a professional image which was not traditionally associated with their industry. In addition to these measures the company also decided to concentrate on improving internal efficiency and quality as a means of strengthening their commercial position. The company have outlined this aim in the mission statement (Figure 3.1):

> The Fortes Company Mission Statement is:
> 'To delight our customers with the excellence of our products and the quality of our service and to return value for money to those who have invested in the company.'

Figure 3.1: *Fortes' mission statement*

MANAGEMENT TRAINING

With the help of an external consultant, Fortes identified that one of their key stumbling blocks to achieving competitive advantage was the fact that they had an inconsistent style of management. The top management had a *laissez-faire* approach to leadership, which was often found in family-owned companies, and middle management on the shop floor tended to be autocratic. This had contributed to the development of a blame culture and an atmosphere of mistrust, which the management were determined to rectify. Under the tuition of an external facilitator the company embarked on a training programme which helped to teach management a number of crucial skills. These included leadership skills, decision-making, problem-solving techniques, presentation skills and also developing and facilitating teams.

Fortes were lucky that they had a relatively young and well-educated management who were willing to learn and were enthusiastic to pass their newly-acquired knowledge down through the company. After this initial training programme the majority of subsequent training has taken place in-house and is usually delivered by a member of the management team. The management team includes the three directors as well as the general, technical and quality managers (see Figure 3.2 on page 87 for details of Fortes' organisational structure).

The management team have developed a very 'hands on' approach to learning, and training usually takes place in an informal setting. This approach has helped learning to become embedded in the culture rather than been seen as an 'add on'. Because a number of employees work long hours and irregular shifts, it is important that training is scheduled in such a way that it is not too time-consuming or intrusive. The management team have gained confidence in their ability to lead the change processes. They are very visible on the shop floor and they operate an open door policy, which means that staff can approach them directly with any questions. This has helped to build up a more open environment in terms of communication and trust.

INITIAL CHANGE PROGRAMMES

Table 3.1 gives a brief illustration of the major changes the company has undergone since 1989. These have included structural changes such as evolving the organisation from a hierarchical to a flatter functional team-based structure, as well as strategic changes which have involved the commitment to quality standards and increasing skill levels.

Table 3.1: *Process of change at Fortes*

1990	Move to exclusively supply the airline industry
1993	ISO9002 accreditation
1994	Membership of British Deming Association
1994	Management training in TQM principles
1994	Flattening of organisational structure
1994	Production Manager job role devolved to newly-formed Team Leader positions
1994	Training for team leaders in functional team-working skills
1994	Cross-functional teams called Quality Improvement Process Teams set up on an *ad hoc* basis to deal with internal problems
1995	Membership of CIRCA CI Network
1993–1996	Implementation of Investors In People standard, which the company achieved in October 1996

INTRODUCING QUALITY STANDARDS

In 1992 the company, with the help of external consultants, introduced ISO9002. The Managing Director had attended a seminar on quality and standards and decided that this was the way forward for Fortes.

First, some members of the management team visited a number of companies in order to learn how they had gone about gaining accreditation. The next stage was to gain the support of other managers within the company and to get everybody to measure the different processes within their area of work. This activity helped to identify procedures, define the different elements of the various job roles and give everyone a common set of guidelines around accept-able standards and procedures. Each section compiled a list of the various job descriptions within that area which were included in the company's procedures manual. The procedures manual is used as a checklist to audit the company and evaluate systems. In October 1993 the company gained ISO accreditation.

Devolving the responsibility for auditing

In October 1992 the General Manager and the Quality Manager attended a course to learn how to audit the different procedures within the company. Internal audits now take place every six months and external audits are conducted annually. Originally all of the auditors were from the senior management team but this caused some problems as individuals felt they themselves were being criticised rather than the process.

Since October 1995 a new auditing team has been set up which includes team leaders and front-line staff, who received their training in-house, and are qualified to audit all areas within the company. All auditors volunteer for the responsibility through the company's e-mail system or by approaching a member of the management team directly. The auditing team con-sists of three front-line staff, one team leader and one manager. Monthly meetings take place in order to keep up to date with each other. The implementation of ISO9002 has helped to increase the general level of awareness in the company, people are more inclined to see their job roles as part of a process rather than in isolation, and the regular carrying out of audits ensures that standards are maintained.

TQM

The next stage of the learning process was the introduction of Total Quality Management in 1994. This programme had a number of objectives which were compatible with the company's business aims and included:

☐ Flattening the organisational structure.

☐ Incorporating quality into everyday work activities.

□   Encouraging teamworking and improvement activities in both functional and cross-functional situations.

Influences in implementing TQM

The initial motivation for introducing Total Quality was as a means of reducing customer complaints. The Managing Director also saw that TQM could play a role in driving change and help to build up a culture which was process-oriented and built around problem-solving and teamwork.

Around this time the company joined the British Deming Association (BDA) as the Managing Director wanted to adopt this approach to quality. The Deming approach advocates rooting out defects and developing an understanding of processes. These aims had been partially achieved by the application of ISO standards. However, some of the human factors, in particular those relating to quality, still needed to be developed and enhanced, in particular creating an environment where there is a 'no blame' culture and encouraging cross-functional working. Initially there was some resistance to change, particularly at middle management level, but as benefits such as reduction in staff complaints and a reduction in staff turnover began to emerge, this resistance was overcome.

The Deming and Crosby philosophies provided the theoretical basis for change and commitment. But as the company became more confident they began to develop their own framework for change. This period represented a major learning phase for the company, in particular the management team. The Deming philosophy advocates that a strong message about quality is understood by everyone in the organisation, and this message is usually passed down through management. Therefore, the managers had to undergo training in order to be able to effectively pass that message to staff.

The company also referred to various sources of help in order to benefit from experience and expertise. These include the Department of Trade and Industry's booklet on best practice benchmarking,[11] together with several visits to companies with a reputation for best practices in TQM.

[11] *Best Practice in Benchmarking*, published by the Department of Trade and Industry as part of the 'Managing in the 90s' series.

In 1995 Fortes joined the CIRCA CI Network at the University of Brighton which gave them access to other companies who were committed to implementing CI. Fortes also introduced some elements of the Crosby philosophy, such as zero defects and the Price Of Non-Conformance, which involves identifying the cost of *not* getting a product or a service right.

ORGANISATIONAL STRUCTURE

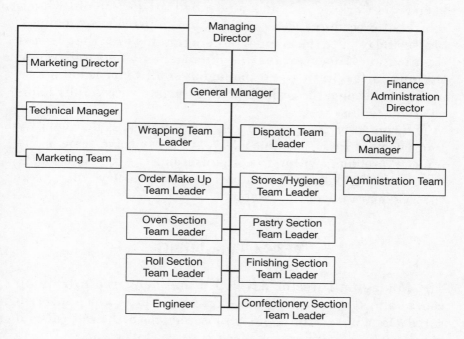

Figure 3.2: *Fortes' organisational structure*

In November 1994 the company went through a delayering process and reduced organisational layers from six to three levels (Figure 3.2). The first change was to establish the position of Managing Director as a formal role. In the previous structure the role was shared between three managers which caused some problems, for example gaps in communication and procedures. The appointment of the Managing Director has helped to focus the company towards a common set of goals and procedures. It was also around this time that the Production Manager left Fortes and the company faced a major challenge at team leader level.

The Production Manager's job was divided between the team leaders. The fact that the team leaders had greater responsibility and control has helped to solve the problem of a communication bottleneck which had been created at the level of Production Manager.

Adapting to the new responsibilities at team leader level was made easier by the fact that the functional teams were established and working well and, since the introduction of ISO, job roles and procedures were outlined in the procedures manual. Staff could refer to the manual if there was any area that needed clarification. However, just as management had undergone training in facilitating and managing staff, team leaders also needed to develop these skills to help them to successfully manage their teams.

The company then set up voluntary teams, called Quality Improvement Process teams (QIPs), to try to solve some of the internal problems within the organisation. The first QIP teams were set up in late 1994 and early 1995, and they will be discussed separately in this chapter.

TEAM TRAINING

The Managing Director developed and delivered a training course aimed at management and team leaders which incorporated elements of the TQM philosophy, both theoretical and practical. The training took place in three stages:

1. team leader training;
2. the opportunity to work within their own teams;
3. the opportunity to work on cross-functional problem-solving teams (QIPs).

The theoretical elements focused on gaining support and consensus that attention to quality and team-building was the way forward for the company. The second phase of training gave the teams the opportunity to develop some of the practical techniques associated with TQM. The majority of these tools were aimed at improving learning and training in a cross-functional, as well as functional, team situation.

The Managing Director customised a toolbox – the **Fortes Quality Toolbox** – which would provide staff with techniques and advice about how to deal with certain situations. Examples include:

- How to work effectively as part of a team.
- How to use problem-solving techniques.
- How to measure processes.
- Advice on how to deal with your internal supplier.
- How to identify opportunities for improvement.

The toolbox also contains information on which individuals within the company staff could refer to for specialist information, for example, to obtain details on training courses and NVQs.

OUTCOMES

The main change which occurred as a result of the team-building exercises was an improvement in the atmosphere, which became less tense and autocratic on the shop floor. The training, which took place for two hours per week over a ten-week period, was delivered to the team leaders. However, some problems occurred due to the fact that the programme had been influenced by CI implementation at other companies. Therefore, amendments had to be made to make it less rigid and more appropriate to the Fortes way of working. The company started introducing their own training material and the development of the 'Fortes problem-solving toolbox' (as outlined above) also helped to overcome some of these barriers to learning.

Suggestion Scheme

At one stage the company introduced a suggestion scheme which involved ideas about opportunities for improvement being submitted to management. However, so many ideas were being submitted that the management team could not process them all.

The scheme was disbanded and the company decided to manage improvement ideas through formal problem-solving teams called Quality Improvement Process teams.

Although the disbanding of the suggestion scheme removed the formal channel for submitting ideas, it appears that individuals are still putting forward ideas informally by taking advantage of the managers' 'open door' communication policy, or through the e-mail system. This system has proved quite successful and ensures that all ideas are brought to management's attention.

QUALITY IMPROVEMENT PROCESS (QIP) TEAMS

The Quality Improvement teams were set up in order to deal with specific problems as they occurred. Over a ten-week period, two hours per week were put aside to solve problems. After a problem has been identified the people who need to be involved are brought together to solve the problem and review the outcome. At the time of writing there were 21 improvement teams in place across the company looking at a variety of issues. For example, one team drew up a procedure for welcoming visitors and showing them around the different sections in the company; another team is looking at the development of recognition certificates.

Communication Sheets

Some of the teams involve just one section of the company and some involve all areas.

A special form, called a communication sheet, is displayed on a notice board in the canteen which names the team leader, coach and other members of the team; describes the issue they are working on; and outlines the progress and outcomes to date. The sheets are updated on a weekly basis.

Examples of some of the projects

One team reduced a two-man job to a one-person job, which has saved the company 50 man hours per week. This was achieved by designing a new bag that fitted into the delivery baskets which could be filled and sealed by one person, rather than its more cumbersome predecessor which had to be filled and tied by two people. Another team was brought together to look at ways of reducing staff turnover. In 1996, staff turnover was down by 57.7 per cent.

STAFF RECRUITMENT

The system of recruiting front-line staff on an informal basis, for example by contacting friends and ex-employees when vacancies arise, has been replaced by a more rigorous procedure. Vacancies are advertised in the local paper and successful candidates must go through a formal application and interview process. Details of applicants who were short-listed but were not successful are kept on file to refer to in the event of future vacancies. This has helped the company to ensure that they are getting the most suitable employees and has contributed to the decrease in staff turnover.

PROBLEMS WITH QIPs

In the beginning it was found that the same people were taking part in the QIPs. These tended to be the 'quality champions' at both team leader and front-line level. The management team encouraged others to become involved but felt that if joining the teams did not remain voluntary, they would return to the autocratic culture from which they had been slowly moving away. There were also problems with some of the teams running out of steam and not finishing the projects in a conclusive way. In addition, there is a tendency for team leaders to focus on their own problems within a cross-functional team rather than taking a holistic approach to problem-solving. One of the reasons appears to be that teams are not using the problem-solving tools and techniques effectively and the Quality Manager has identified this as an area for improvement. At the time of writing all the teams were being coached by a member of management rather than the team leader. The team leaders do not feel confident yet in their ability to lead and this is a behaviour which the company plans to develop.

Some of the teams tend to be quite competitive, which does not help cross-functional working. The approach to team leader training has been to concentrate on introducing problem-solving techniques. However, the training did not try to develop a consistent style of leadership or values for team leaders. As a result some of the team leaders are still imposing a rigid style of leading which was a feature of the old culture at Fortes. Certain measures are being taken to overcome these problems such as the introduction of IIP, which should encourage multi-skilling, communication and job rotation.

RECENT DEVELOPMENTS

Just-in-Time (JIT) techniques

In the last six months some of the product ranges have introduced Just-in-Time techniques. This was an important development for a company that produces over 286 lines of perishable goods. The procedure is only suitable for some of the easier-to-control lines and was introduced due to customer complaints arising from mould problems which resulted from the very hot weather in the summer of 1995. The decision to introduce JIT resulted from a brain-storming session between the General Manager (of production), one of the team leaders and the sales teams.

This shows that the company has made some progress in the introduction of cross-functional team-working. The benefits accruing include tangible savings due to:

☐   no over making of goods;
☐   no remaking of goods;
☐   no goods going off.

Quality Club

Any member of staff can join the Quality Club which meets after work on an informal basis. The MD leaves the onus on individuals to become involved, rather than forcing the issue. The Quality Club includes people from the British Deming Association, who give support and advice on how to introduce quality systems. Often guest speakers will attend (both from within and outside the company) to discuss any issues of interest. Statistical Process Control was introduced six months ago and, using the expertise of the Quality Club, a paper has been introduced which offers advice to managers and team leaders about best practices in implementing SPC. The club also serves a social function, as it provides the opportunity for people from different areas in the company to get together outside a work situation.

Meetings take place every six months to discuss financial issues and to benchmark progress using quality data. It appears that measurement has been introduced in every area, but is not being recorded thoroughly.

Investors In People (IIP)

The company is committed to the implementation of the Investors In People Standard, which is being supported by the Sussex Training and Enterprise Council.

Three years ago, in 1993, IIP was identified by management as a major strategic aim for the company. Each section in the company is categorised by different skill requirements. The team leader regularly tests each team member and, when appropriate, credits them with all the skills in that section. This should help to improve the skills level in the company. The team member can then request that they are moved to another section in production, in order to increase and build on their existing skills.

A training matrix is produced for each section, showing the required skills within each section and the current skill levels of each member of the team. The employee and the team leader meet to review a training plan based on the matrix. The training plan outlines planned and actual dates for the training of each team member. Once a month the team leaders meet with the Personnel Officer to review team training achievements and update training plans. It is the responsibility of the individual's team leader to implement the training programme. The Managing Director provides access to and funding for external training courses when an employee requires additional support. Every six months the team leader reviews the training agreement with the employee. In October 1996 Fortes were accredited with the IIP award.

An evaluation form is used to evaluate both 'on the job' and external training. These forms are then updated to monitor the impact of training and assess further training needs.

National Vocational Qualifications (NVQs)

A number of employees at all levels have undertaken to increase their skill level through studying for NVQs. This is a voluntary initiative, but the company hopes to see the NVQ programme becoming integrated into the general company-wide training scheme. There is a proposal to train team leaders in the skills of assessment which should help them in their role of assessing and developing staff. The company has also outlined some generic competences they wish to strive towards, including the development of 'good relationships, attitude and teamwork'. In less than six months the company expect to see the first NVQ candidates receiving their awards.

The managers really encourage learning and training at all levels.
Office employee

CULTURE

The cultural change at Fortes is ongoing: however, they do seem to have made progress in improving communication between the different levels in the company.

I notice management are making more effort to go around the shop floor and talk to people.
Front-line employee

In addition to operating an 'open door' communication policy, the Managing Director outlines any free slots in his diary during which employees are invited to come and speak to him about any issues or concerns they have. This sheet is put up on the notice board and staff can pencil in appointments.

In October 1996 the company sent out a questionnaire to all
staff under the banner of 'Aims, Principles and Values', asking
them how they wanted to be treated, and what standard of
behaviour and level of cooperation they expected (from themselves and others). The objective of this exercise is to develop a
standard of expectations and behaviour throughout the company to which everyone can adhere.

NEW PRODUCT DEVELOPMENT (NPD) AND 1996 BUSINESS STATEMENT

Fortes are now looking at making improvements to, and developing, the existing product range. This is being achieved
through continued development of cross-functional teams and
the movement away from structural thinking to systems thinking and team thinking and working.

The new business statement in 1996 identified that the company needs to establish an environment where improvement
can take place. Customers' expectations have changed and the
company needs to become more customer-oriented and to ask
employees for opinions and input. The company is aiming to be
a learning organisation, which will involve training team leaders to effectively make decisions rather than management dele-
gating actions and decisions. Deciding on a particular style of
leadership, which the company wishes to cultivate, should help
to overcome some of the problems of a blame culture and some
of the teams being managed in an autocratic style.

FORTES – REVIEW OF IMPLEMENTATION

Key points

- The company adopted a 'top down' approach to change
  which was driven by senior management.
- The aim of the change process was to train staff to have
  a common approach to quality, and to improve teamworking.

- ■   The focus was on improving internal efficiency and quality in order to strengthen the company's commercial position.
- ■   The original approach drew heavily on external sources, such as the Deming and Crosby philosophies, but as internal expertise and knowledge developed the programme was adapted to fit in more with the company culture and internal way of working.
- ■   Senior management developed a strong style of leadership and as a result were more confident in actively leading the ongoing change process.

Summary

Fortes is in the early days of CI implementation and, to date, the company has experienced a number of tangible benefits. The introduction of quality systems and procedures have improved internal efficiency and productivity. Customer satisfaction has improved, with a 50 per cent reduction in customer complaints, and the company is gaining a reputation throughout the industry for delivering a quality service.

CI also brought Fortes intangible benefits such as improved company culture and teamworking. The company has recognised that CI cannot be directed by management alone and that responsibility for change has to be devolved to other levels in order to have a long-term effect. One of the key learning points in this case is that employees have to be given the appropriate tools, training and opportunity for meaningful involvement in order to play an effective role in the change process. As part of the learning process the company is now looking at new ways of developing a culture which is open to learning and helps devolve responsibility to all levels.

Case 4
VEEDER ROOT ENVIRONMENTAL SYSTEMS EUROPE (UK) – MARKET HARBOROUGH

Veeder Root Environmental Systems Europe (UK) carries out the European operations of Veeder Root UK (a flagship company of the Danaher Corporation based in Washington DC, US).

OVERVIEW OF CASE

Over the last four years the whole company has undergone a number of transitions and learning cycles. Central to the change process at Veeder Root is the introduction of CI, which has been driven by top management.

At Market Harborough the company has successfully implemented CI through the application of two key strategies: first, by devolving responsibility for achieving business objectives to all levels; and secondly by encouraging employees to input ideas. The company has not introduced a formal CI programme, but incremental improvements (kaizens) occur regularly in both team situations and on an individual basis. As well as the tangible benefits CI has achieved, it has also contributed towards creating a more self-sufficient and innovative workforce.

BACKGROUND

Although CI at Veeder Root is creative and largely uncontrolled, we can see where improvements are needed, and policy deployment drives the process.

Site director

The company has two locations within the UK. Sales for electronic gauging systems, found on petroleum sites, are based in their London headquarters. Manufacturing, distribution, service support and sales of non-electronic products are based at Market Harborough in Leicestershire. The Market Harborough site was originally family-owned and produced basic gauging systems for measuring the contents of underground petroleum tanks. In 1992 Veeder Root purchased the company from Microlec. Veeder Root also manufactures gauging equipment and their product ranges include electronic systems for leak protection and stock control. Customers for this type of equipment include ESSO and Shell as well as supermarket chains such as Tesco and J Sainsbury. The company maintains 60 per cent of the US market share and 90 per cent within the UK.

POST-TAKEOVER

When the company took over the premises at Market Harborough major reorganisation and changes took place. These included the following:

☐ concentration of all manufacturing operations at Market Harborough;

☐ concentration of sales and marketing for traditional products at Market Harborough;

☐ an investment programme and considerable reorganisation of the Market Harborough site.

The company, pre-takeover by Veeder Root, had a traditional approach to working with a mechanistic style of management. Among the first changes to take place was to foster a new climate where people were given the freedom to experiment and learn from their mistakes. Other elements of the acquisition plan included plans to improve standards, quality and staff training – see Table 4.1.

Table 4.1: *The challenge of change*

Redefine responsibilities at all levels	Focus on customer needs
Introduce modern management systems	Introduce modern manufacturing techniques
Introduce Quality Assurance systems through ISO9001	Introduce Supplier Partnerships
Introduce major training plans for managers and staff to become multi-skilled	Prevention of errors

DRIVER FOR CHANGE

The introduction of CI at Veeder Root was motivated to a large extent by policy and work practices at Danaher Corporation. In 1992 the UK board members visited the parent company where they were impressed with the high levels of employee involvement in implementing change, through 'kaizen', to improve processes. These activities involved 'solving' rather than just 'identifying' problems, and their involvement was largely 'improvement'-, as opposed to just problem-, oriented. The approach taken in the American company gave the UK subsidiary a framework in which to introduce the principles of CI. Under the guidance of the parent company, and with the help of a Japanese consultant, Veeder Root began their CI journey.

CI TRAINING

Training was introduced using the expertise of an external consultant as well as examples of best practice from the parent company in America. In the first instance two of the managers were trained as facilitators, and eventually four to five people across the organisation were trained in this role. The facilitators encouraged involvement in the kaizen teams, which were set up to tackle areas in need of improvement across the company. The kaizen teams operated on an *ad hoc* and informal basis. People were encouraged to become involved in teams in which they could make a positive contribution. This was achieved by giving individuals the opportunity to participate informally in a team, by observing, learning and asking questions and, finally, taking a more active role. This has helped to gain support for the kaizen way of working which has now become a part of everyday working, and it operates on an informal basis without monitoring or supervision.

In the early to mid-1990s Veeder Root, along with a number of other UK companies, had undergone a variety of initiatives aimed at achieving competitive advantage. These included lean manufacturing, cost reduction, faster delivery time and introducing standards and procedures, for example through ISO9001. The next phase of change was quality-driven and focused on increasing customer satisfaction.

Recent impetus for change focuses on employee involvement and creating a 'learning organisation'. This is probably one of the most difficult stages in the improvement cycle in terms of both implementation and quantifying outcomes. However, Veeder Root had an advantage in that it was a small company with an open-minded workforce, and this has hastened the process of change.

Management support

One of the main tenets of CI is to give employees the opportunity to learn new skills and develop. In Veeder Root one of the employees (who was an unskilled worker) was encouraged to develop some IT and computer skills. This particular worker asked to be made redundant rather than learn a new skill which he was afraid he did not have the ability to master. However, through training and management support the individual gained the required skills and has since adopted a more responsible job role, which requires a greater level of skill and capability.

Information technology

Information technology has helped to speed up a number of processes by generating data which helps the company to assess performance. For example, both customer complaints and ISO standards are now on-line. All training in the use of information technology took place in-house and all staff are trained to analyse their work performance based on computer-generated information. This is done on a monthly basis to help monitor how well targets are being met.

Approach to CI

In the early days the company recognised that success would not happen over night, and that aiming for 100 per cent improvement company-wide was neither realistic nor practical. Therefore, the company decided to focus on making incremental improvements across as many areas as possible.

> CI looks at any aspect of our business to try to make small improvements, 5 per cent here, 2 per cent there, which helps keep our attention focused on everything. We're not looking for 100 per cent improvement, our culture is too bogged down in this, we just need to improve and get modest gains, going back to the drawing board and looking forward all the time.
>
> *Hugh Chapman, Site Director*

The logic of improving efficiency by 5 per cent each year is demonstrated by Figure 4.1, which reveals how incremental improvement over a long period of time can add up and help to keep the competition at bay.

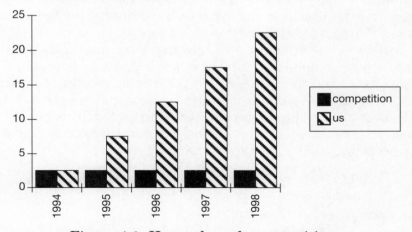

Figure 4.1: *How to beat the competition*

POLICY DEPLOYMENT

The corporation has outlined their key objective as follows:

> To achieve world class excellence in customer
> satisfaction by continuously striving to improve
> quality, service, delivery and cost.

Veeder Root is implementing this objective through policy deployment, which means devolving responsibility for meeting business aims throughout the different levels within the company. While policy deployment is a corporate objective for the group as a whole, each site has the autonomy to implement it in the way most appropriate to their way of working. The advantage of using policy deployment as a means of introducing CI, or 'kaizen', is that each of the business aims has an impact on different parts of the company. This helps to ensure that the improvement activities are linked to specific targets and strategic aims, which makes them more meaningful to individuals by giving them a greater sense of ownership.

Devolving responsibility

Annually the board identifies the key business aims for the company and outlines the expected performance for the coming year. The board will first draw up a broad aim – for example, 'we want to be world class and improve customer satisfaction'. There are elements of this statement that can be applied to every area and the management team come together to ensure there is consensus about the targets. Each manager then takes these objectives into their own work unit and splits it into six or seven items to which the section can contribute. Examples of generic targets include the following:

□   to improve quality;
□   to exceed expectations;
□   to put the customer first;
□   to ensure best practice;

☐   to meet promises and commitments;

☐   to reduce costs and increase efficiency.

In order to achieve the objectives and create the kind of culture where 'everything can always be improved', the company ensures that the targets are achievable: for example, an expectation of 8 per cent increased productivity or 5 per cent reduction of rejects over a six-month period.

Monitoring policy deployment

The items/targets are quantified, put on a chart and monitored every month. Feedback is given and reasons for slippage or not achieving targets are explored.

The advantage of policy deployment is that it sets up targets and drives the company in the direction the board wants to go. It also gives freedom at the individual level, while ensuring everyone is driving towards a common goal. The objectives are recorded on a 'Policy Deployment Matrix' to which all staff can refer. The policy deployment targets at the time of writing this case were set in September 1995 and came into force in January 1996. These are posted around the building within each work area and in communal areas, such as on the company notice boards. Targets are assigned to individuals and kaizen teams are set up as necessary to work towards meeting those targets.

For example, an employee identified that the cost of production was too high at £500. A kaizen team was set up which succeeded in reducing production costs to £115 in two attempts. The kaizen teams capitalise on the skills of the people with the relevant expertise, regardless of their level in the company. For example, the Site Director and front-line staff are currently working with customers to help develop and modify a new product.

PHILOSOPHY FOR CHANGE AND PROFESSIONALISM

The philosophy for change at Veeder Root is based on a code of behaviour which encourages people to make improvements, without trying to force employees to contribute. The onus is on management to lead and encourage people to put forward ideas (see Table 4.2). Guidelines on how to communicate with people are illustrated in the following table. Veeder Root have helped to make the change process more visible by formally recording their expectations in terms of exchange of information and the scope of projects.

Table 4.2: *Management of people*

Management of people is about:

☐　Management of the unknown and of fear.

☐　Leadership – focused direction and execution.

☐　Direct and open communications.

☐　No false promises.

☐　No false or patronising rewards.

☐　Training, development, multi-skilling/tasking.

☐　Promotion of team-work and flexibility.

☐　Visible display of information.

☐　Sympathise when things go wrong.

Enablers

The kaizen teams are usually set up in such a way that maximum benefit is gained from shared knowledge and skills. Usually there are six team members, consisting of two people who know the process and four others who are not from the same work area but who can make some useful contribution. The team members come together to look at the process and set up charts to allocate responsibility. If possible, the teams try to restrict the time spent on solving a problem to two days.

Some of the kaizen activities that take place are more informal and are linked more to local improvements in performance than strategic goals. Examples include improvements by employees to their own work area. Employees are given the freedom to arrange their work areas in a way that ensures maximum efficiency and comfort.

The following points outline the approach to project management at Veeder Root which help to define the scope of projects and how the process should be managed and recorded.

Guidelines on managing CI projects

- Pick a tool you understand.
- Pick a project which is easy and where success is assured.
- Involve a number of people from different disciplines.
- Train project team in tools being applied.
- Record existing process and record changes.
- Ensure project is completed and regularly audit and maintain new methods used.
- Publish the benefits and acknowledge progress and success.

Staff training

'Staff training, teamwork and the introduction of simple management systems have resulted in significant improvements in the Market Harborough company's performance.'[12] The majority of training takes place in-house. The site director has a very 'hands on' approach to training, and gives a training course in basic word-processing to staff that require it. The company has developed a training plan in which each individual has a number of modules to achieve. There is no formal system for monitoring individual performance except through the measurement of the targets set on the Policy Deployment Matrix. The company also takes an outward approach to identifying gaps in skill levels by bench-marking performance against other companies. Membership of the CIRCA CI Network gives Veeder Root the opportunity to meet other network companies to compare experiences and share ideas.

Increase in employee skill level

Since 1992, the company has managed to build up employee skill levels and develop a highly flexible workforce who can cope

---

[12] Article printed in the *Leicester Mercury* in November 1994 in relation to Veeder Root achieving the Company of the Year Award, organised by *Commerce* magazine.

with change. In the early days operators performed a small number of functional tasks, usually about four; now each worker can perform approximately 32 tasks, which can be applied across a range of functions within the company. This flexibility has been driven partly by the aims of meeting customer delivery times and improving performance.

Cross-functional job rotation takes place on an *ad hoc* basis. An operator will often help out in the sales function, when they are understaffed or inundated with customer calls. This approach to work helps to create a greater awareness of customer relations, as well as giving direct feedback to the front-line staff.

IMPROVEMENT IN EFFICIENCY

We can see advantages so we are convinced, but many are dismissive and do not see the value in small things. Those who are convinced bring about a change of attitude.

Hugh Chapman, Site Director

The improvement in efficiency has been brought about by a gradual attack on all areas rather than through major change. This has resulted from giving employees the opportunity to specify and implement changes in their workplace which make the job a bit easier. The majority of changes have taken place within the production area, and they are summarised in Table 4.3. Some of the improvements have been implemented by individuals and some by kaizen teams. The majority of ideas are small, but may still have had an impact on the company as a whole.

Other examples of CI initiatives include displaying kanban cards in an internal assembly which act as instructions for assembling parts, rather than getting instructions from supervisors. Everyone is trained in each cell and operators can move around between the different cells. This has helped achieve a number of benefits, including simplifying the process, reducing stock levels, improving quality and giving individuals more control over their work area so they can now carry out their tasks without requiring supervision from the works manager.

Table 4.3: *Improvements made by individuals and kaizen teams*

Improvement to	Old system	Improvement	Area	Implemented by	Result
Available storage space	No designated place to store probes	Design of customised racks	Stores	□ Kaizen team □ Engineering and stores	□ More space □ Reduced cycle of activity and time wasted
Redesign of work space	Single function work areas	Design of multi-purpose work bench	Packing	□ Kaizen team	□ Simplified task □ Increased efficiency
Redesign of work space	Operator working from three different desks	Redesign so functions could all be operated from one desk	Manufacturing	□ Kaizen team	□ More pleasant and efficient work area
Automating processes	Hand-written labels on products	Barcode system introduced	Manufacturing production	□ Kaizen team	□ Speeds up process

Equally, the fact that tasks are clearly illustrated in different work areas has helped increase job rotation and flexibility without requiring in-depth training. These open stations are simple to run which means that anyone can do the work there. More people can work together in this area if the company is inundated with orders, which helps to ensure that the three-day order delivery system is met.

A group of operators decided that they wanted to redesign their electronic PCB board area to be more efficient. They went to an electronics show and selected the parts that they wanted, which were the most appropriate and cost-effective. Management invested the money and bought the carousels for holding stock on-line and the employees redesigned their whole work area. Carousels are loaded with different programmes presenting operators with parts they require, thereby eliminating the searching process and speeding up assembly of electronic boards. The area was then fitted with a home-made extraction system used to filter out odours and fumes through a fan (which used to be a old toolbox!). As a result of these changes all manufacturing times were reduced by 50 per cent. This is a good example of how employees used their initiative and understanding of their work area to implement an improvement which made the work area more efficient, comfortable and environmentally sound.

KEY ATTAINMENTS FROM THE KAIZEN TEAMS

The main benefits from the kaizen teams include:

☐ greater understanding by employees of processes and how job roles fit into the overall structure and aims of the company;

☐ turnover has increased by 47 per cent;

☐ overdue customer orders have reduced from 430 to five over 18 months;

☐ order response time has been reduced from eight weeks to three days;

☐ customer satisfaction is in excess of 90 per cent;

☐ process time has been reduced by up to 88 per cent;

☐ product costs have been reduced by up to 79 per cent;

☐ 35 per cent saving on space utilisation.

SUCCESS FACTORS

The Site Director attributes the success of kaizens to the fact that change is brought about as an ongoing process with modest targets rather than adopting a 'company-wide 100 per cent improvement' approach. The projects which are chosen often rely on input from a number of disciplines and the results are 'quick and dirty', so people can see the improvement early on. This helps to ensure that momentum is sustained and projects are completed, as well as ensuring people remain motivated. The philosophy of 'incremental improvement' as an ongoing process seems to have taken root in the company. In fact, the

Managing Director remarked that he was not aware of all of the changes that have been implemented, as people seem to have made a habit of seeking out ways to improve things without looking for recognition:

> Quality has improved as people know what they are doing now so it is easier to monitor when things go wrong.
>
> *Hugh Chapman, Site Director*

Reduction of inventory was a UK corporate objective which has been very successfully achieved, and now the Market Harborough site acts as a role model for the European subsidiaries of how to introduce 'best practice'.

Other factors which have helped the company to achieve competitive advantage include simplifying processes and reducing the amount of paperwork generated. For example, in an attempt to abolish all work orders the company now uses many dispatch notes. This piece of paper has numerous functions. It works as a kanban by generating information to downgrade stock levels, as well as acting as an authorisation to manufacture a product. The dispatch note is on-line, which means that all areas of the company can access the information. The company also uses the electronic mail system as a form of internal communication and as an interface between the different departments such as sales and marketing and production.

E-mail

The electronic mail system has also been used as a means of passing on information on correct procedures and practices within the company. For example, when a customer complained about the telephone manner of an individual in the company, correct procedures on how to address customers were e-mailed to all staff which helped to deal with the problem without targeting or disciplining one individual. The e-mail system has helped to speed up processes through bypassing traditional communication channels and getting individuals from different locations directly in touch with each other (for example, the London office interfacing with Market Harborough).

Information sharing

The communication system at Veeder Root is quite simple and straightforward. A lot of information is displayed on the company notice boards. One of the notice boards acts as a sort of recognition or achievement board. This displays photographs, press releases and bar charts showing improvements and reductions, as well as a glossary of terms for visitors. A general notice board displays social events and general news.

The third board outlines more formal company policy and objectives: for example, what needs to be done in the different parts of the organisation; the company's monthly performance, including any indicators of poor performance, such as overdue customer orders; and the Policy Deployment Matrix, which outlines the extent to which targets have been met.

CULTURE CHANGE

The change in culture at Veeder Root has resulted from getting people from different teams and departments to talk to each other, both informally and through the kaizen teams. Attempts are made to involve all staff, both those working within the organisation and field workers such as service engineers.

For example, in 1995 a problem arose between the service engineers and the manufacturing section. One of the company targets was to reduce the amount of faulty parts that were returned by customers from 35 per month to seven per month. This was achieved, but it transpired that the service engineers were not returning parts quickly enough to be able to determine a root cause analysis. This problem took a year to solve as the two sides tended to blame each other. Eventually the management spoke to the service engineers, and the Manufacturing Engineer suggested that they sat down and worked things out together. The engineers and manufacturing sections put their heads together and developed new test equipment, training programmes, and fault analysis techniques which allowed them to identify problems and achieve greater customer satisfaction.

Results

In 15 months a system for prioritising and dealing with faults was implemented and in the intervening time the culture of blame and poor communication between the two different sections had been broken down. The company has also achieved a number of awards over the last few years. These are outlined in Table 4.4 below.

Table 4.4: *Awards and recognition*

1994	Winners of the *Commerce* business magazine company of the year award for 'Manufacturing Excellence'
1995	Manufacturing Industry Achievement Awards 'Manufacturer of the Year'
1996	Department of Trade and Industry 'Insight Company'

VEEDER ROOT – REVIEW OF IMPLEMENTATION

Key points

- The aim of CI implementation at Veeder Root was to develop a culture via training to allow people the freedom to experiment and develop techniques in support of the overall corporate objectives.

- The approach to CI is informal and encourages incremental involvement. Employees in the production area were given the freedom to arrange their work area in a way that ensured maximum comfort and efficiency, and this has helped to create a culture of experimentation.

- The CI activities are focused on improving internal efficiency and cross-functional working. The targets are modest and ongoing and results from projects are visible early on. This approach has helped ensure that the momentum is sustained and it encourages people to remain enthusiastic.

- The opportunity for meaningful involvement is enabled through policy deployment. This means that all employees have targets and objectives assigned to them and this helps to drive CI in work situations.

- Veeder Root has reaped a number of benefits from the introduction of CI. These are measured in terms of statistical outputs, margins and reductions in inventory and operating costs.

- As the CI process becomes an integral part of everyday activities it becomes more difficult to measure the tangible outcomes. Veeder Root is now at the stage where CI can no longer be documented totally in quantitative terms, but it has moved to a level where it is becoming ingrained in the culture.

Summary

As a small company Veeder Root cannot afford to have resources tied up in implementing programmes which work in parallel to daily activities. Therefore, the approach to CI at Veeder Root is fully integrated and there are no formal systems such as suggestion schemes or newsletters to encourage involvement. However, the Site Director plays a very supportive role in the CI process and helps encourage people to make improvements to their work area. There are also a number of enablers in place to encourage involvement, including kaizen teams to tackle specific problems and help share knowledge.

This case provides a good example of CI being introduced in a way which best suits the organisational culture. However, the informal approach taken by Veeder Root might not be as effective in a large organisation which did not have such a highly skilled and flexible workforce. Although the informal nature of CI activities indicates a high degree of autonomy and freedom, some advantages may be lost if good practice is not captured, and learning by sharing information may not be fully utilised.

Case 5
LUCAS DIESEL SYSTEMS (UK)

Lucas Diesel Systems (LDS) is part of Lucas Industries plc. The Sudbury plant produces components for diesel injector systems – filters, nozzles, injectors and delivery valves – and also makes complete diesel injector kits.

OVERVIEW OF CASE

This case focuses on the changes that took place at Sudbury. After a sustained period of growth in the 1970s the company, and the industry as a whole, went into decline due to a reduction in sales and increased competition.

CI was introduced into the factory in the late 1980s following radical reorganisation of the production system. The new system of flexible specialisation involved wide-ranging organisational change, which was important in establishing an infrastructure that was conducive to CI. Initially, the main vehicle for involving employees in improvement activities was the introduction of group problem solving teams, known as Process Improvement Teams (PITs). Building on the success of these, the emphasis subsequently shifted toward smaller improvements that employees are empowered to make themselves. The initial programme of radical change was successful in transforming the site from a loss-making factory into a centre of excellence, with operating costs cut by £11 million per annum.

The implementation of CI has ensured that the momentum of change has been maintained through incremental improvement. Tangible benefits alone accruing from CI activity are worth £884,000 annually to the company. However, intangible benefits, particularly in terms of cultural change, have been equally, if not more, important. External recognition of Sudbury's achievement is reflected in the number of awards received, including *Management Today*'s 'Britain's Best Factories' and quality awards from Ford New Holland (1989), Ford of Europe (1991) and the New Holland Fiat Group (Fiat bought Ford New Holland) Farm and Construction Machinery Sector Quality Award 1993.

In 1994, Lucas Industries employed around 46,000 employees and had an annual turnover of £2487.9 million. LDS accounted for 7000 of these employees and £450 million of this turnover. Following group restructuring in 1991, the site at Sudbury was one of ten manufacturing sites across six countries within LDS, all of which report to a Divisional Office in Blois, France. In 1994, LDS Sudbury employed around 1000 employees and had a turnover of approximately £40 million.

The Sudbury site has a wide range of products, particularly in comparison with its sister plants in France. Since the major reorganisation in the mid-1980s, when many of the support functions were centralised, operations at the plant are largely manufacturing-based, with few commercial activities.

BACKGROUND

Initial facilities at Sudbury were set up in the 1940s and a further site was acquired in the 1950s as production expanded. However, this still proved inadequate to cope with the volume of demand and a new factory was constructed on a greenfield site in 1964/5. The factory incorporated the latest in manufacturing design and technology and, at the time, was one of the most automated factories in Europe.

With a sharp rise in demand for injector products during the 1970s the subsidiary nearly doubled in size and the workforce increased to 2400. The factory's output was largely destined for two major UK original equipment manufacturers (Ford UK and Perkins Engineering), with the remaining 30–40 per cent produced for the after-market. Consistent growth in output led to the addition of three extensions to the site.

MOVE INTO CRISIS

Output and sales turnover both continued to grow until the late 1970s from which point they went into decline, and the real level of turnover fell by 64 per cent between 1977 and 1983.

External factors

Initially, the pattern of declining sales was attributed to changes in the external environment, characterised by a general fall in UK commercial sales and, more specifically, the sharp decline in market share of British commercial trucks and tractors, which accounted for the majority of LDS's sales. Having defined the problem as an external one, the management response was a strategy of reduction in real prices (ie not raising them in line with inflation) in an attempt to maintain its market share and production volumes. The real unit selling price fell by 46 per cent between 1977 and 1984. This strategy of price reduction was largely ineffective, however, since output also reduced over the period, highlighted by a drop in the level of real turnover of 64 per cent between 1977 and 1983. The company had merely plunged into deeper crisis and was on the brink of bankruptcy. It was only then that attention shifted to internal factors.

Internal factors

The manufacturing processes at LDS were originally designed around a system of functional specialism, whereby similar machinery and processes were grouped into specialised functional areas and work in progress transported between these. The system of functional specialisation was designed to maximise the advantages of large-scale production and minimise the perceived disadvantages created by a relatively high degree of variety in LDS's product range. A minimum batch size of 3000 was set in order to minimise set-up and changeover costs between product runs, which tended to be very time-consuming.

This system of manufacturing was becoming increasingly at odds with the nature of demand, both within the automobile sector and across industry at large, which was shifting toward demands for greater variety and innovation, but without having to incur the penalties of a higher price or longer delivery lead time. Alongside this was a growing emphasis on the importance of non-price factors in satisfying customer demand. To deal with these challenges, many automobile assemblers were adopting the Just-in-Time philosophy and, consequently, were demanding smaller batches and shorter lead times from their suppliers.

INTRODUCTION OF A NEW PRODUCTION PHILOSOPHY

LDS was not alone in facing declining competitiveness. From the mid-1970s onwards, similar problems had affected the group as a whole, although it was the automotive subsidiaries that were particularly hard hit. In 1981, for the first time ever, Lucas Industries plc made a loss.

The crisis facing the group convinced senior management of the need for drastic action and, in 1982, Lucas Headquarters devised a programme to bring about radical and wide-ranging organisational change. The programme consisted of establishing task forces within the subsidiaries, who were charged with developing a Competitive Achievement Plan (CAP) to assess the potential of the subsidiary and plan a course of action. It was envisaged that developing a CAP would involve benchmarking against competitors and identification of customer needs.

Using the outcomes of these assessments, a plan would then be devised for improving performance over a three-year period. To assist these task forces, a team of systems engineers from Lucas Engineering & Systems were made available to act as consultants to plants wishing to undertake change, although this assistance had to be purchased. The team of consultants was led by John Parnaby, a leading academic. In preparation for the task that lay ahead, the consultants had conducted a study of Japanese manufacturing success and it was the outcome of this study that formed the basis for the approach subsequently adopted by LDS Sudbury.

Due to the extent of the crisis at LDS, the management team was forced to take action prior to the formalisation of these corporate level strategies for reorganisation. In 1981, the management team at Sudbury was told that, unless they regained profitability, the subsidiary would be sold off or closed. The management had little option but to take up the challenge and, at the end of 1981, a multi-disciplinary task force, consisting of management representatives, technical staff, shop floor workers and consultants, was set up to identify the problems facing LDS and to find and implement solutions. To assist the task force in the reorganisation, they were put through a comprehensive training programme. As a result of LDS's early involvement in reorganisation and its subsequent success in doing so, the subsidiary played a key role in defining a model for change for the group as a whole and thereby helped the Lucas group to restructure its global operations.

Identifying the problems at the Sudbury plant

The task force at Sudbury recognised that problems lay in the internal organisation of what was becoming an increasingly outdated production system. In particular, there was a need to cope with the increasing product variety — around 410 different nozzles, 200 different injectors, and 100 different filter assemblies. More specifically the following problems were identified:

- long and variable lead times;
- slow responses to changes in demand;
- batch sizes larger than customer order sizes;
- stock turn to sales very low (high stocks and work in progress);
- poor quality;
- ownership and responsibility vague;
- high indirect/direct labour ratio.

In addressing these problems, the task force adopted four key objectives:

1. design a manufacturing system which satisfies customer needs with respect to price, performance/quality and delivery;
2. effect a real reduction in operating costs;[13]
3. do the above with minimal investment;
4. create an environment where people matter.

APPROACH TO CHANGE

Key points

■ Reorganisation of manufacturing operations resulted in a move towards smaller batch sizes and more customer-oriented production.

■ The plant was divided into three business units to support the different product families which included nozzles, filters and injectors.

■ A new 'craftsperson' grade was introduced, which helped to create more versatile and multi-skilled employees. This was supported by an on-site open learning centre.

■ Benefits accrued from the changes include a reduction in costs by £11 million and a substantial increase in employee productivity and satisfaction.

The solution adopted involved the redesign of manufacturing operations and accompanying changes in the organisational infrastructure to support this. Underpinning the reorganisation was the recognition that automation was not a solution in itself. This shift in approach was partly fuelled by a senior managers' visit to Japan early in 1983. The purpose of the visit was to purchase state-of-the-art machine tools; instead, the experience brought home the message that success lay in the reform of the

[13] A goal was set of reducing real operating cost by 25 to 30 per cent.

production philosophy rather than in a technological fix approach.

The move away from a technology for technology's sake approach is reflected in patterns of fixed investment in LDS. Over the period of reorganisation, fixed investment fell from a high of 14 per cent of sales in 1977 to less than 4 per cent of sales between 1983 and 1986. Fixed investment did, however, rise again towards the end of the restructuring, in 1987, when new types of flexible equipment became appropriate. Apart from this, as far as possible, the company utilised existing equipment and sold off items which became surplus to requirements. It was found that most equipment operated effectively under the new regime of small batch sizes.

Redesign of product operations

The reorganisation centred on a new philosophy of flexible specialisation, based on the maximisation of production flexibility and a drastic reduction in the size of production runs. (Minimum batch size was reduced from 3000 to 300.) To make this new system cost-effective, an emphasis was placed on reducing changeover times. Instead of the previous supply-driven approach of making to stock and forecast requirements, the new philosophy was a customer-oriented one, where demand acts as the trigger to production. In order to reflect this philosophy, production facilities were reorganised into 'cells', based on the concept of families of parts. Three separate product types were identified (filters, nozzles and injectors) and the plant effectively split into three separate business units based on each of these product types. Within each of these business units, a number of cells (21 in total) were set up to support the product varieties. A fourth unit, Delivery Valves, was later created when business from the Finchley in-line pump factory was transferred to Sudbury.[14]

---

[14] In 1994 this was merged with the Nozzle Unit.

Production cells

Creating the cells involved the regrouping of equipment from specialised departments containing similar machines and functions to equipping each individual cell with the equipment and processes to make the complete product, eg for cutting, grinding, turning, drilling, washing, etc. However, a detour was required for the heat treatment process, since this was the only process which was not effective under the new principles of economy of scope. Two support units were set up to provide site service and business functions to support the cells (145 people to support total plant of 1270). The distribution of these support staff is shown in Table 5.1. The support functions were also relocated so that they were nearer to the manufacturing process.

Table 5.1: *Distribution of support staff*

Service	Number of employees
Site services	
Provision of utilities	23
Personnel	20
Tooling	21
Overall plant management	8
Business functions	
Marketing support	12
Financial services	8
Product engineering	25
Business systems	4
Quality control	24

The transition to the new production system was not easy and in fact it took nearly two years after the solution was identified to introduce the first pilot cell, in February 1984. Much of this delay was due to the problem of trying to convince one member of the task force that the cellular layout was viable. The pilot cell took seven months to become fully operational and it was only when this was successfully operating, with clear results, that other cells were set up.

The manner in which the reorganisation was carried out demonstrates initial moves to operationalise the task force objective of 'creating an environment where people matter'. A participative approach was taken in setting up the new cells, whereby employees at all levels participated in a series of multi-disciplinary task forces around the core of what was to become the production cells. These groups were responsible for defining the configuration, size and equipment needs of the cell. The aim of this participative approach was to promote 'ownership' and responsibility for improvement beyond the remit of senior management. In doing so, LDS had started to sow the seeds for cultural change toward teamwork.

INFRASTRUCTURAL CHANGE TO SUPPORT NEW PRODUCTION PHILOSOPHY

The task force recognised that the redesign of production operations alone was insufficient to meet the reorganisation objectives since, under the new philosophy, success was also dependent on creating the appropriate organisational structure and infrastructure to support the new system of production. Many of the changes implemented reflected moves to increase the degree of employees' responsibility over the production process and an organisational commitment to developing the potential of its employees.

The main changes to support the new production system were in the following areas:

☐ a reduction in the levels of organisational hierarchy;
☐ a moving toward multi-skilling;
☐ a commitment to training and education;
☐ the development of a new communication system.

Organisational hierarchy

Prior to reorganisation, there were seven levels of management and at least seven demarcations of setter/operator. This was simplified as three levels of management – factory manager, unit manager and product manager – and two categories of production workers, 'manufacturing craftsperson'[15] and 'operator', as illustrated in Figures 5.1 and 5.2. The product managers were responsible for specific production cells and reported to the relevant unit manager. In addition to the managers involved directly in production, the post of Operations Manager was created to oversee all support staff.

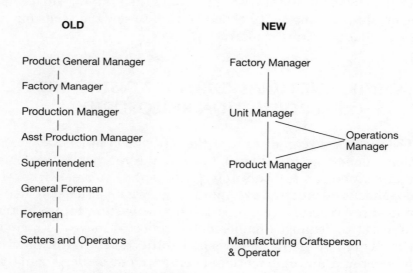

Figure 5.1: *LDS hierarchy pre- and post-reorganisation*

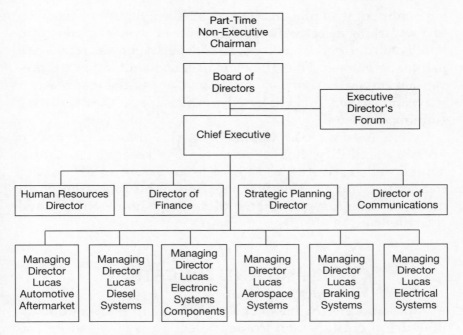

Figure 5.2: *New organisational structure*[16]

MULTI-SKILLING AND FLEXIBILITY OF WORK PRACTICES

The creation of a new category of production employees, the 'manufacturing craftsperson', represented a move toward multi-tasking/multi-skilling. These workers, initially constituting around 10 per cent of the workforce, were trained in a range of tasks that were previously carried out by individuals of different demarcations – such as machine setting, work scheduling, tool maintenance, preventive maintenance, quality control and problem diagnosis. Many of these tasks were previously seen as indirect tasks which were outside the remit of production staff, performed instead by production support staff. Of particular importance was the move to make quality the responsibility of production workers, under the principle of 'right first time'. The

[16] Information on the parent company is drawn from Loveridge (1988 and 1989). The history of LDS and details of the reorganisation are drawn largely from Hoffman and Kaplinsky (1992).

old quality control function involved 230 employees in checking and reworking defective items. Under a new system of control of quality at source, the quality control department was reduced to just 24 employees. Thus the emphasis had shifted toward prevention rather than cure. For each cell, one of the manufacturing craftspersons would be largely responsible for the day-to-day running of the cell.

By expanding skills in this way, the aim was to create greater flexibility. It also reflected the recognition that a skilled and motivated workforce is an essential element of competitive success. However, creation of this role required an intensive training programme to develop the new skills and competencies.

TRAINING AND EDUCATION

All workers were eligible to apply for training for the new manufacturing craftsperson grade. Selection was based on the results of eight hours of tests – which included mathematics and spatial abilities. Anyone who achieved more than 400 points out of a possible total of 800 could go on to the next stage where they were assessed by an interview panel on a range of criteria, including the individual's 'openness to change'. Those who did not pass had the opportunity to utilise the plant's 'Open Learning Centre' (consisting largely of video-based material) or could ask for release for off-plant study. Access to training and education through the Open Learning Centre and off-plant study arose from initiatives at the corporate centre, reflecting a corporate-wide commitment to training.

The Open Learning Centre at Sudbury was one of 16 set up at various Lucas sites around the country. It offered a number of courses in subjects such as electronics, foreign languages, general education, management and administration, basic numeracy, presentation and communication skills, quality and software training. This was complemented by the Continuing Education and Training programme, which allowed employees to undertake a range of courses/qualifications at various levels, ranging from City and Guilds to PhDs. As well as training in areas directly related to manufacturing, there was a wide range of support for personal development.

The overall take-up of training opportunities for the group was around 60 per cent. As LDS continued to change, workers whose jobs had become obsolete could be directed to the Open Learning Centre to retrain in new skills which would enable them to take up new positions within the organisation.

Individual training development triangle

Every employee was encouraged to take a series of training and development steps outlined in their individual training development 'triangle', developed in conjunction with the training, quality and product managers to ensure that training needs were linked to future business requirements. Each step in the training plan aimed to help individuals to work more flexibly and perform other tasks in the organisation so, for example, operators can eventually become manufacturing craftspersons by gaining the skills to do any job along their line. Through this training and education programme LDS was able to create an environment where people are generally aware of the need for training and are willing to take training steps to improve their performance and position.

Communication

It was recognised that if workers were to take greater responsibility there was a need to change attitudes, among both management and workers. Historically, relations at LDS were typified by an 'us and them' culture, with workers feeling 'no one tells us what is going on' and 'no one listens to us'. Traditionally, communication between management and workers was top down and through indirect, union channels. Management felt that this often resulted in workers receiving a distorted message. The communication also tended to be confrontational in nature, centred around negotiation of areas of conflict, rather than the communication of information essential to effective production.

An overhaul of the communication system and the development of more open and honest communication was an essential component of the reorganisation task. By explaining everything that was going on within the factory and encouraging feedback, the aim was to enhance employees' understanding of the production process and their role within it. In addition to giving employees information about the progress of the company, mechanisms were also introduced to keep them informed of the progress of their team (cell).

New communication channels

The task force recognised the need for a number of new channels of communication, the main components of which were as follows:

☐ a standard set of slides to be used in presentations to groups of workers to explain the key tasks of the reorganisation;

☐ each shift began with the cell manager talking through the day's production with the work team;

☐ a monthly meeting of about 15 to 20 people from all levels including senior managers, senior stewards, manual workers and union representatives to discuss progress to date in the reorganisation programme;

☐ the introduction of an in-house newspaper, *On Site*, to pass on information to the workforce;

☐ twice-yearly meetings attended by everyone (in groups of around 200 workers) to give an overview of progress and future plans. The employees would then be broken up into sub-groups and put together written questions to submit to the management team;

☐ a Communication Board for each cell to display information on quality, production cost, stock-turn and productivity (plus other information).

Since the initial overhaul of the communication system, the communications framework within the company has not remained static. It has been regularly reviewed and amended as necessary.

Help scheme

The introduction of the new communication system was not without its problems. For example, there were initial problems in developing effective communication between shop floor workers and product managers in charge of cells. Some product managers proved unwilling to hold regular meetings, to such an extent that problems were not being resolved. The help scheme was introduced to overcome this, whereby individuals were able to request feedback on any issue or problem which they felt had not been effectively or satisfactorily dealt with through other communication channels. Several staff were chosen to act as confidential intermediaries, passing the form to the appropriate individual who would be required to reply within a specified time. The transaction was completed when the originator of the help form was satisfied with the reply and signed it off to this effect. Management argued that a measure of the success of the scheme was the decline in its usage – from around 100 help forms outstanding at any one time in the early days of its operation to between five and 10 outstanding help forms by the early 1990s.

Reward system

Prior to the reorganisation the company operated a payment system based upon piecework, which reflected the then strategic priority of maximising production. Under the new production system a different method of payment was required since the original one conflicted with the new emphasis on quality. Consequently, a new biannual 'factory-bonus' incentive system was introduced for all workers, based on a combination of quality and quantity. Factory performance in cost reduction was one of the factors contributing toward this bonus scheme.

In addition, other changes were made to the remuneration system which were conducive to the cultural shift that LDS was trying to achieve. For example, the concept of single status was introduced with respect to benefits such as pension, sickness benefit, holidays and incremental pay scales.

BENEFITS OF THE REORGANISATION

The main thrust of the reorganisation was implemented in the mid-1980s. During this period, the manufacturing site shrank from two factories employing 1600 people to one factory employing around 1000 people. The reduction in the size of the workforce was largely achieved through a programme of voluntary redundancy and early retirement. In fact, only ten compulsory redundancies were made.

The reorganisation was clearly a success, in terms of both the tangible and intangible benefits. Operating costs were reduced by £11 million compared to a capital expenditure of just £1.5 million, which was spent mainly on reorganising existing plant and machinery.

Tangible benefits

Other tangible benefits of the reorganisation included:

☐ reduction in the proportion of indirect workers from 41 per cent in 1978 to 14 per cent in 1990;

☐ increase in labour productivity, with units per worker more than doubling by 1989;

☐ reduction in overall lead time from 21 weeks to four weeks;

☐ increase in stock turn (ratio of annual stock turnover to end of year stock) from four in 1982 to 11.1 by 1989;

☐ reduction in the physical space required for production from 204,000 feet in 1982 to 162,000 feet in 1989 (which made it possible to sell off one of the sites);

☐ reduction in scrap levels from 2.3 per cent to 1.8 per cent of sales volume between 1983 and 1989. This led to both improved customer satisfaction and financial savings. The new system encouraged workers to 'find scrap' rather than hiding defective production;

☐ production costs reduced by 20–30 per cent (in real terms).

Intangible Benefits

In terms of intangible benefits, the reorganisation had improved the quality of jobs and atmosphere of the factory. In general, employees liked the greater variety of work and gained greater satisfaction from being able to see a product through from start to finish. The new communication systems played a key role in developing a committed workforce.

In fact, the infrastructural change introduced during the reorganisation played a vital role in creating an environment 'where people matter', that was conducive to, and supportive of, CI. The very mode of reorganising was intended to foster a sense of involvement and ownership amongst shop floor workers, first by involving them in the reorganisation task (through the task forces), secondly, by giving them greater responsibility for the production process (eg through taking on responsibility for quality and maintenance) and thirdly, by creating more channels for bottom-up communication.

'Old habits die hard!'

Despite the success of the factory reorganisation, the management recognised the danger of slipping backwards and reverting to behaviour and practices associated with the old system. For example, managers found that work-in-progress stock levels had a tendency to creep upwards toward pre-reorganisation levels, which reflected the discomfort that workers felt working with the low levels required by the new system. Resistance was experienced when managers attempted to deal with these types of problems. Consequently, it was acknowledged that a one-off step change would be insufficient to maintain and build upon the initial progress that had been made; systems were needed to support continuous progress.

Supplier pressure

The main spur to action, however, came from supplier pressure. A quality systems survey by its largest customer in 1988 found LDS lacking in its employment of statistical methods to support quality management. The Quality Executive decided that the best way to rectify this would be through the introduction of multi-disciplined teams who would employ relevant statistical techniques in structured problem-solving activities.

PROCESS IMPROVEMENT TEAMS (PITs)

As a result of supplier pressure, the Quality Executive, working with external consultants, designed a programme to implement Process Improvement Teams (PITs). Initially, two pilot PITs were set up, one in the Injector Unit and one in the Nozzle Unit. Following early signs of success with these pilots, a further eight PITs were started a few months later, without waiting for the pilots to conclude. In order to achieve and demonstrate management commitment at the outset, members of the management team took part in the first PITs.

Some initial resistance was experienced from both employees and the unions. Amongst the workforce there were fears that involvement in the PITs would ultimately lead to job losses. The introduction of problem-solving teams also revived some of the negative feelings associated with experiments with quality circles some years earlier. These problems were minimised through open communication and the involvement of a trade union representative in the PIT training courses.

Clear guidelines were laid down to support the operating procedures of the PITs. The Quality Department was given overall responsibility for managing the vehicle and ensuring that the teams followed the guidelines. Topics for PITs were generally identified by managers, although the idea may have arisen as a result of complaints or suggestions from shop floor staff.

Once a project was defined by management, it was then passed over to the product manager of the relevant cell who would put the team together and nominate a team leader. The project teams were usually cross-functional, drawing together volunteers from the wider product team and co-opting 'experts' on to the team (four to ten people in total). Other people could be brought into the team for specific tasks as and when required. In some cases, a particular customer or supplier would be included in the team.

Training

Once a team had been put together, it would attend two days of off-site training covering:

- □   evolution of manufacturing concepts;
- □   introduction to the philosophies;
- □   customer/supplier relationships;
- □   the Quality Improvement Process (QIP);
- □   the seven diagnostic tools.

The QIP aspect of the training covered a formal problem-solving cycle (identification, selection, solving, implementation and review) and a number of tools (flow charts, histograms, Pareto analysis, scatter diagrams, control charts, attribute sheets and cause and effect diagrams), details of which were included in the toolkit booklet that accompanied the training.

The training was delivered by an external consultant and comprised a roughly equal mixture of tutoring and practical exercises. The end result of this training was the development of an interim plan of action for the initial stages of the project. The team members would then return to the workplace and progress the project over the next two weeks, trying out the tools. Much of this time would be spent in collecting the necessary data to be analysed in the second training session. The fact that employees were given the opportunity to try out what they had learned in a real situation, very shortly after they had been trained, was seen as essential to the effectiveness of this training – otherwise, there is the danger that the training is forgotten before people have an opportunity to use it. As one manager commented, 'You can't change people unless you let them play with the new toy first'.

The second stage of training, a further two days off-site, covered:

- □   discussion of problems encountered;
- □   the essentials of teamwork;
- □   establishing performance measures;
- □   introduction to process mistake proofing;
- □   creating the project plan;
- □   preparing the presentation;
- □   presentations to senior management.

Although this was the last formal training session, the teams were free to request further training in any other tools that suited the needs of their particular project. At the end of the second phase of the training, the team would present the project plan, including objectives, parameters and Gantt chart to the senior management and then receive the go-ahead to complete the project.

Projects

Projects typically ran for between six and 18 months and consisted of a weekly team meeting (one to two hours). Throughout the life of a project, regular review meetings were held with the site management team and the project team presented their progress made since the last meeting. This provided an opportunity to review the terms of reference of the project and amend them as necessary. Progress was also recorded in the project log.

On completion of a project, a formal presentation was made to management, demonstrating the findings and the results achieved. A project file was then created containing all the information about the project, to be kept as a reference point to avoid 'reinventing the wheel' in the future. To celebrate the conclusion of the project, the team were invited to a buffet lunch with the management team and guests at which all team members were presented with a leather folder and a certificate. The achievement of the group was also publicised by displaying details of the project in the foyer for a month and by including the project in *On-site* magazine. These also provided mechanisms by which the learning could be transferred to other projects and other parts of the organisation.

Identifying benefits of projects

Identifying the tangible and intangible benefits accruing from a particular project would be part of the team's task and covered in the training. The team would be taught to identify 'a stake in the ground' – a measure of the current levels of scrap, reject rates, tooling costs and so on. Throughout the project improvements would be recorded – tangible savings calculated and intangible benefits identified. For example, one project achieved a reduction in reject levels from 18 per cent to 2 per cent. This represented a saving of £135,000, plus benefits of reduced variability, improved gauging, improved method of manufacture and improved process control. Another project was successful in reducing the scrap rate of injector deep hole drilling, saving £28,000, with intangible benefits of a more satisfied customer and increased productivity.

By January 1995, 50 teams had been commenced, of which 39 had reached their conclusion. In addition to a wide range of intangible benefits in areas such as team-building, personal development, customer satisfaction and operator involvement, the improvements implemented by the PITs also resulted in tangible savings of around £884,000 per annum for the company (as verified by the company's accountants).

LINK BETWEEN PITs AND CI

Although the initial impetus in setting up the PITs was not directly linked to the concept of CI, their role in introducing CI has since been recognised at all levels within the company, both formally and informally. The ongoing improvement activities of the PITs enabled the organisation to build upon the process of organisational and cultural change begun with the reorganisation.

Across the organisation, employees at all levels had a clear perspective of the CI philosophy, supported by visible commitment from the senior management, who devoted around a half-day per week to CI-related activities. To help communicate the concepts behind CI and its role within the organisation, Core Business Training was introduced in 1993 as a two-day programme to be attended by all employees. The training also encouraged employees to make any suggestions and take part in PITs.

Bottom-up communication was enhanced by the introduction of the Q1, Q2 and Q3 quality meetings. These operated by feeding information from the shop floor up to management and proved to be an effective way of making everyone aware of improvement needs. The two-weekly Q1 meetings consist of product managers and individuals from their line who meet to review performance data and improvement action plans. This feeds into the Q2 meetings of Unit, Product and Operations managers at which improvement plans and performance data are reviewed on an aggregate basis. Finally, this information is reported to the Q3 meeting of the management team.

COMMITMENT TO CI

The commitment to CI is now formally recognised as a central facet of the organisation's strategy, featuring prominently in a range of documentation, particularly the 'Quality Policy and Philosophy'. This was based upon four main commitments:

1. customer focus (internal and external customers);
2. CI;
3. teamwork;
4. Statistical Process Control (SPC).

Other activities which formed part of the wider strategy were:

□ customer perception analysis, which consists of a monthly despatch audit during which the management team look at the product (including packaging) from the customer's point of view;

□ component quality review, in which a sample of a new product is measured and tested and Pareto analysis used to identify which areas have the greatest potential for improvement;

□ ISO9002 programme;

□ mistake proofing programme;

□ system audits, whereby an in-house team audits the systems twice a year;

□ supplier quality development programme.

Suggestion scheme

The commitment to CI led to revived interest in the Lucas suggestion scheme. This was originally introduced as a head office initiative in 1921, but was given little attention until the late 1980s when its potential contribution to CI was recognised and efforts were devoted to promoting widespread usage of the suggestion scheme. After overcoming initial problems with slow response rates, with the number of suggestions awaiting a response reduced from 200 to a maximum of five in any unit, this met with some success. By 1993, Sudbury had the highest ratio of suggestions per worker in whole of the Lucas Group. Figures 5.3 and 5.4 show the overall numbers of suggestions and the number of suggestions per employee.

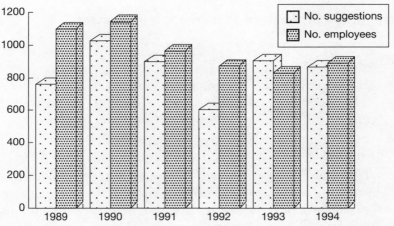

Figure 5.3: *Number of suggestions and number of employees*

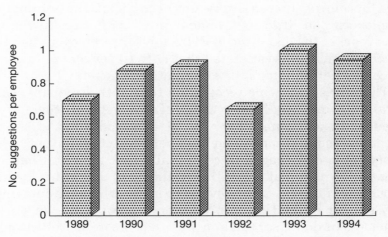

Figure 5.4: *Number of suggestions per employee*

Implemented suggestions could earn the originator a monetary reward up to a maximum of £750 (in 1994). Overall, the monetary rewards represented around 10 per cent of the savings resulting from implementation of ideas in the first year. A non-monetary 'merit' award was given to those suggestions which were well thought-out but not implemented. A formal appeals procedure was introduced to ensure that decisions were fully justified.

Recognition of the need to increase involvement

Key points

- Although the PITs had acted as a catalyst for change and CI, the company needed an alternative vehicle to increase CI involvement at an individual level.
- In 1992, 'Little Improvements From Everyone' (LIFE) was set up.
- The LIFE initiative was deemed successful but, as improvements are increasingly becoming a more integral part of everyday work, it is difficult to measure its success in isolation of other factors.

Despite the achievements of PITs and the suggestion scheme, it was becoming increasingly apparent that the majority of employees had little involvement in CI activities. In the first four years of the operation of PITs, only 260 employees had been involved and it was estimated that only 10 per cent of the workforce had participated in the suggestion scheme.

There was a growing recognition that, if the company was to attain significantly higher levels of involvement, there was a need for an additional CI vehicle. More specifically, the management wanted to create an environment based on 'kaizen', where everyone is encouraged to continually look for small improvements they can make. Central to this was the desire for CI to become an integral part of everyone's job, rather than having to pay out for every tiny improvement (as with the suggestion scheme). In doing so, the aim was to promote more bottom-up involvement (so far much of the CI activity had been management-led) and individual ownership of work. To take this forward, a steering committee, with representatives from all levels, was set up to explore methods of getting people involved.

Little Improvements From Everyone (LIFE)

The outcome was the introduction of LIFE, Little Improvements From Everyone, at the end of 1992; a vehicle based on simple ideas that individuals could implement themselves in their local work area. This represented an important distinction between LIFE and the suggestion scheme, with LIFE representing greater empowerment because employees had the autonomy to implement their own small improvements immediately, without seeking prior approval (other than to discuss it with their immediate supervisor before making the change). Thus the formal submission of the improvement was made *after* the idea had been implemented. It was hoped that this would overcome some of the problems associated with the suggestion scheme, particularly the possible demotivating effect when proposals were not followed up. Originally, the steering committee planned to set up a specific budget to support LIFE improvements. However, it was decided that the initiative would be more effective if funded from existing budgets, since this would reinforce the message that CI was part of normal organisational activities.

Conflict between LIFE and the suggestion scheme

Although LIFE was intended to overcome some problems with the suggestion scheme, there was the potential for new problems to arise due to conflict between the two schemes.[17] For example, it was felt that people might prefer to use the suggestion scheme for any ideas since this offered the opportunity of a financial reward. To overcome this problem, it was decided that employees would be allowed to put more substantial LIFE improvements into the suggestion box retrospectively. However, it was felt that the greatest source of motivation and reward for LIFE suggestions would be to see them being implemented, rather than as suggestions for other people to implement.

[17] There was no scope for replacing the suggestion scheme with LIFE since it is a Lucas group initiative.

The first step in implementing LIFE was to train the management team and to gain their total commitment. This was followed by a pilot scheme in which 120 volunteers, drawn from all areas of the factory and from all levels, were trained. The LIFE training consisted of a half-day session off-site. The training highlighted the difference between LIFE, which was improvement-orientated, and existing CI vehicles which tended to be problem-orientated – the message being, 'don't wait for a problem to occur before trying to improve'.

Monitoring and measuring

In order to monitor progress and measure the success of the scheme, all employees were issued with a small blue pocketbook in which they could record the improvements they had implemented. The form was deliberately kept very simple to encourage participation and avoid people being put off by the bureaucracy. The records of improvements made were collated on a database by the quality management team and the monthly progress charted. The results were published in the quality brochure and the most recent ideas displayed monthly with photographed examples accompanied by the question, 'Can any of these be implemented in your area?', to encourage the transfer of learning.

Examples of LIFE improvements

One LIFE improvement was to replace coffee urns at meetings with much smaller Thermos jugs, which led to a substantial saving in the amount of unused coffee; another eliminated a safety hazard by running cables in conduit in the conference rooms. From the initial 120 people trained, 250 improvements were implemented, between January and June 1993.

By January 1995, 485 out of a total of 999 employees had been trained (49 per cent of the workforce) and, in all, 854 improvements had been implemented over the first two years of its operation. However, the actual number of improvements implemented was thought to be considerably higher since manage-ment found that not all employees were bothering to fill in the blue forms. Whilst this made it difficult for management to mea-sure the success of the initiative, it did indicate that CI was increasingly becoming an integral part of organisational life.

RESULTS

By January 1995 the new CI vehicle was judged to have been largely successful. A high number of improvements had been made, more people were involved and individual empowerment had increased. The scheme had also attracted considerable interest from Lucas's customers, many of whom had made less progress with this type of scheme.

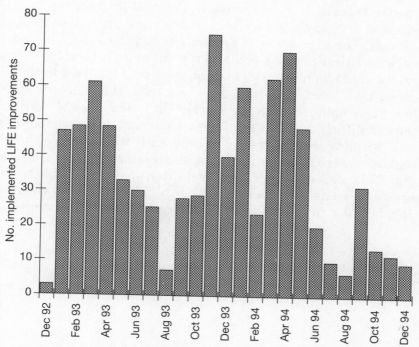

Figure 5.5: *Number of implemented LIFE improvements. January 1995: 49 per cent of employees trained (485 of 999 employees)*

Setbacks to sustaining interest in LIFE

However, a number of important challenges remained. The bimonthly breakdown of implemented LIFE improvements (Figure 5.5) indicated that each training session generated peaks of improvement activity, often followed by declining numbers. This posed the biggest challenge: how to sustain the momentum of LIFE. In addition, they were finding that there were pockets of high activity with many others still not getting involved. Increased management commitment and more push from local management were identified as key areas for improvement in order to demonstrate the importance of LIFE activity and ensure that attention did not stray to other issues which are seen as having a more important impact.

Major expansion and restructuring at Sudbury towards the end of 1994 also adversely affected the roll-out of LIFE, reflected in the low numbers of LIFE improvements over this period. In order to cope with a sharp rise in demand in the French subsidiaries, an increasing amount of business was pushed out to Sudbury. The expansion in production and the associated shift in the nature of the new demand toward more high volume, low variety products has led to a major restructuring. In addition to setting up a number of new lines and cells, the Delivery Valve Unit was combined with the Nozzle Unit. The pace of demand made it difficult to release production staff to participate in LIFE training. Furthermore, to cope with the expansion more employees were taken on, bringing the total workforce to around 1000. This placed an even greater burden on the available training resources as the new staff not only needed to be trained in LIFE but also in other aspects of the quality and CI systems.

LUCAS DIESEL SYSTEMS – REVIEW OF IMPLEMENTATION

Key points

- Lucas Diesel Systems adopted a well-paced reflective approach to change, which was supported by a three-year plan. The company evaluated the impact of any changes before rolling out the initiative; for example, a pilot scheme took seven months to implement and changes to the production system took two years to roll out. As a result the company was able to gain maximum learning from the changes as they were occurring.

- A cross-functional task force team was put together to help to establish what the problems were. The introduction of this support team ensured that ownership of the change programme went beyond the remit of senior management.

- The CI programme aimed to improve internal operations and meet strategic needs, such as satisfying customer requirements.

- Radical changes were introduced prior to CI implementation. For example, business units were set up to support product families. Also, the introduction of a new grade of skilled employee was supported by an Open Learning Centre on site. This 'people-focused' approach to change has helped to develop a culture which is conducive to CI, as well as ensuring that the organisation is equipped with the skills needed to maximise competitive advantage.

- Top-down and bottom-up mechanisms of communication, including regular feedback from different levels of team meetings, has helped ensure the accurate and timely transfer of information.

Summary

To a large extent it has proved difficult to clearly identify benefits that can be attributed to CI, since CI at Sudbury was not pursued in isolation but formed part of a wider strategy. However, managers were convinced that CI has been an important contributory factor in the consistent improvement in the performance of the subsidiary.

In terms of the level of CI activity itself, measures of the numbers of PITs, suggestions and LIFE improvements indicate significant levels of involvement, and benefits to the company worth £884,000 per annum are attributed to PIT activity alone. This is in addition to many intangible benefits, such as improved customer satisfaction, team-building and personal development.

An interesting learning point is that the company originally went to Japan intending to invest in technology, but instead came back with the philosophy that central to the change process was the need to invest in people – not technology!

The Lucas Diesel Systems case is a good example of how a planned approach to change, using mechanisms to regularly review and evaluate the impact, can ensure maximum effect and enable the CI programme to be strengthened by ongoing adaptation as the need arises. Another important lesson from this case is how timely training, relevant to the work context and using appropriate tools, helps newly-learned skills and knowledge to take root.

Case 6
HOSIDEN BESSON LIMITED

Hosiden Besson Limited, a manufacturing company based in the south-east of England, designs and manufactures acoustics, plastics and electronics for the telecommunications market. It is a subsidiary of the Japanese Hosiden Group, which specialises in the design and manufacture of components for the IT industry and has annual sales of over £600 million.

OVERVIEW OF CASE

After a period of decline in the late 1980s, Hosiden Besson Limited began to concentrate on improving marketing and manufacturing processes. Complementary to these objectives was the plan to encourage ideas and involvement at all levels of the organisation. In 1992 Hosiden Besson introduced CI, which was managed by a steering committee.

In 1994 two Teaching Company Associates were employed to manage the development of CI on a full-time basis. Initial projects focused on the development of team-building and problem-solving. Following this, the initiative was rolled out to encourage involvement at an individual level (Little Improvements From Everyone – LIFE). To date, this has proved very successful in breaking down communication barriers and encouraging initiative.

The company has reaped both tangible and intangible benefits from CI and is currently in the process of creating a greater link between CI and the company strategy in order to meet overall business objectives.

BACKGROUND

The Hosiden group has 12 subsidiaries, nine of which are in south-east Asia, two in Europe and one in the US. Hosiden Besson Limited is, however, the only manufacturing subsidiary outside south-east Asia, since the German and US operations are sales-based subsidiaries.

Hosiden Besson Limited has core expertise in three main areas: acoustics, injection moulding and PCB mounting and assembly. It manufactures a variety of products, ranging from consumer electronics components to complex telecommunications devices. The company employs around 550 people spread over four sites on the south coast: the main site at Hove, East Sussex (which encompasses two factories); two nearby in Portslade, East Sussex; and the fourth at Ryde, Isle of Wight. The Head Office, containing Personnel, Sales, Marketing and R&D functions, is located at Hove. In 1996 sales reached approximately £32 million.

HISTORICAL DEVELOPMENT

The company was founded in 1957 by AP Besson to produce a miniature hearing aid but by the 1970s, after going through a number of ownership changes, the company had become a subsidiary of Crystalate Electronics plc. To optimise resources, in the 1980s, Crystalate merged two other companies with Besson. The logic behind the merger was that each of these companies had British Telecom as their main customer.

Changing competitive environment

> *Key points*
> Hosiden Besson experienced a decline in competitive position in the late 1980s due to the following factors:
>
> - slow reaction to changes in technology and the marketplace;
> - low levels of investment in the company;
> - internal inefficiencies such as poor delivery and quality performance;
> - competition from south-east Asia.

Up to the late 1980s AP Besson had a high market share of sales of acoustic components to BT. It was a profitable business, operating within a stable environment with good margins. However, as BT started to become more cost- and quality-oriented, Besson was faced with a number of challenges.

As Besson's competitive position began to decline, internal inefficiencies became increasingly obvious, reflected in poor delivery and quality performance in the late 1980s. Further, the company's inability to respond quickly to the new challenges in the marketplace was compounded by management and financial problems within the parent company. Consequently, levels of investment in Besson were very low. From 1986 onwards, the company started to make a loss and its survival began to look very uncertain.

Takeover by the Hosiden Group

By 1990 Crystalate was unable to continue to support the losses that Besson was making and, in March of that year, sold the company to the Hosiden Corporation. Hosiden, in common with many Japanese-owned companies at the time, wanted a European manufacturing base to guard against expected high tariff barriers on Japanese imports to the EU. Unlike the majority of Japanese companies, who established greenfield sites, Hosiden decided to invest in an existing UK operation. It was felt that they lacked the necessary management resources to start up and run a greenfield site. In addition, the investment in an existing business would enable the Group to build upon Besson's range of technical skills and home-grown sales and marketing expertise.

The company experienced the following changes after takeover in 1990:

□ reduction in costs;

□ investment in technology;

□ fostering relationships with new customers in the UK and overseas;

□ development of existing products and the introduction of a new product development process;

□ expansion to the two main sites and acquisition of a new site;

□ flattening of the organisational structure.

Apart from initial restructuring and redundancies, the workforce, who had been expecting a major transformation, saw little immediate change. Instead, the turnaround was a more gradual process. On the operations side, the Hosiden Group took a long-term approach, writing off losses of around £450,000 and giving the management the autonomy and time to demonstrate their capabilities. As the company started to reduce costs and become fitter and leaner, money was made available for investment which allowed the company to take on new technologies such as surface mount technology and injection moulding.

The most significant changes, however, were made on the product and marketing front, instigated by the new Japanese president. He devoted time and effort to fostering new relationships as part of a new customer and product development strategy. This strategy incorporated four main aims:

1. Reduce Hosiden Besson Limited's dependence on one large customer and a large number of small customers. Instead, the aim was to develop business with a greater number of larger companies and a lesser number of smaller companies.

2. Target large original equipment manufacturers as potential customers, develop long-term relationships with them and

then gradually expand the range of products supplied. The Hosiden name allowed privileged access to these major new customers that would not have been possible before the takeover.

3. A new product mix was introduced, based on the concept of product families. This involved the introduction of two to three entirely new product categories. Product managers were designated to look after each product category.

4. A new product development process was introduced.

Remote control devices and hand-free speakers were two of the first new products developed. The hand-free speaker business, supplying Motorola and Nokia, proved to be particularly successful, expanding rapidly from one to three assembly lines. The company began to tap into new sectors of the electronics industry and identify new product areas within these sectors. By the mid-1990s, Hosiden Besson Limited's main markets were identified as:

☐ telecommunications;

☐ mobile communications;

☐ TV, audio and video;

☐ fire prevention and security.

It took some time for these changes to filter through. As the new business was being developed, the pattern of declining sales and profit continued in the first year following the takeover, reaching a low point in the middle of 1991. As an increasing number of new products reached production, the company started to grow. In 1993 profits moved back into the black and in the following year the first significant profits were achieved. Telecommunication (mobile) and consumer electronics products, which were not in the product mix in 1991, accounted for 69 per cent of turnover by 1994. Further, an increasing proportion of the new business was developed with overseas customers such that, by 1995, around 40 per cent of business went outside the UK.

To support the business development activities, from 1992 onwards the company started expanding its manufacturing facilities, with extensions to the Ryde and Hove factories and the acquisition of a new site about a quarter of a mile away from the existing Portslade site. In May 1995, the hand-free speaker production and Siemens car kits operations were transferred to this new site. At the same time, the size of the workforce grew from around 350 in 1992 to 550 by mid-1996.

ORGANISATIONAL STRUCTURE

The company had a traditional hierarchical structure. Problems were reported to managers by staff, and management then took decisions and delegated accordingly. As a result the people at the bottom did not have confidence either in management decisions or their own ability to solve problems. In 1989 changes were made in the production system (from a batch system to flow-lines.) The new production layouts proved to be a success and flow-lines were subsequently introduced in other areas. However, no single production method is applied throughout the factory; instead the organisation of production tends to vary according to what is most appropriate for a particular process or product.

INTRODUCTION OF CI

Key points

■ Establishment of a steering committee.

■ Membership of the CIRCA CI Network.

Initial interest in CI

Over 1992, both Richard Edwards (Managing Director) and Jeremy Evans (Manufacturing Director) became increasingly aware of the concept of CI and the potential role it could play at Hosiden Besson Limited. In September 1992 the Production Department were very busy with a lot of overdue orders. The company were unable to recruit fast enough to get enough shop floor staff so they hit upon the novel idea of getting office staff to

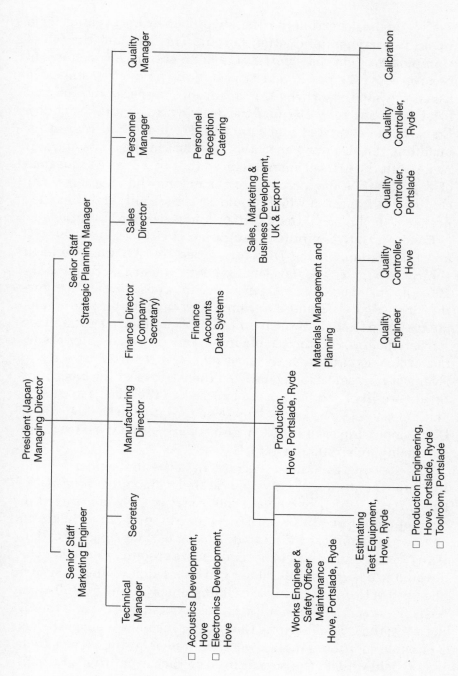

Figure 6.1: Organisational chart – management structure

work (unpaid) overtime on the shop floor every evening for a week, to increase production output. The MD had the job of stamping an item code on the area of an ear-piece which would be covered with a pad in a later part of the production stage. He asked the supervisor why this apparently unnecessary job had to be done. She said, 'Because the drawing calls for it!' Next day, Edwards investigated and found that the original reason for including the stamping operation was 'lost in the mists of time'. As a result the MD became convinced that there were thousands of opportunities for increased efficiency on the shop floor, the cumulative impact of which would be significant, and that they needed to mobilise all their staff to find those opportunities.

Following a five-minute consultation in October, both the MD and the Manufacturing Director agreed that CI was the ideal vehicle to support the development of the business. By January 1993, Evans had set up a steering group, whose brief was to further investigate CI and determine how it could best be implemented at Hosiden Besson Limited. The steering committee consisted of around ten people in engineering or quality assurance roles across the sites, most of whom reported directly to Evans. Evans selected people from these areas on the basis that they were likely to have been exposed to the need for change and, therefore, were more likely to be receptive to the concept of CI. Membership of the CIRCA CI Network also proved useful in enhancing understanding of CI.

The steering committee decided that the first major step in the implementation of CI would be to develop a training package through which to educate the workforce. Evans started to develop this but, due to other commitments, was unable to devote any significant time to it. It soon became apparent that, if any real progress was to be made, more resources needed to be devoted to ensure that it did not run out of steam. Ideally, someone needed to be managing the CI implementation on a full-time basis. Following discussion with the researchers running the CI network, the DTI's Teaching Company Scheme was suggested as a possible solution. Further work on implementing CI was then put on hold whilst attention focused on the preparation and submission of a bid for two Teaching Company Associates.

Preparing the ground — cultural change

Whilst the launch of the CI programme itself was put on hold, an external audit conducted by researchers from a local university highlighted significant obstacles to the introduction of CI within the company, the majority of which were cultural. In particular, the audit revealed a need to reduce the 'us and them' barriers between managers and operational staff. Feelings of being undervalued were widespread amongst the workforce. People felt that no one really listened to them and they received little recognition for their efforts. The 'us and them' culture was reinforced by lack of management visibility.

Although the organisational structure had already been flattened, the hierarchical culture persisted in other ways. For example, communication channels were predominantly top down, with most information disseminated to employees through supervisors. The introduction of a monthly, written team brief to disseminate information about strategy and company performance to employees through the supervisors had done little to improve communication. Some employees simply did not understand the information, whilst others paid little attention.

There were few mechanisms to promote lateral communication and employees had little insight into the operation of the other sites within Hosiden Besson Limited. The few existing opportunities for bottom-up communication were rarely used. For example, a Company Council was held every month/six weeks, attended by a representative from each area of the company who would put forward items or questions from the colleagues in their area and feed back responses. However, many felt that it was not worth putting forward questions as they received little feedback. A number of changes were introduced to help overcome these barriers and smooth the future path of CI:

- A series of inter-site visits for operational staff so that they could see what went on in other sites and meet people from other sites.

- As part of the 'Training School' run for new recruits to help develop the necessary technical skills, a new management slot was introduced where senior managers would tell them about the company. This also provided an opportunity for the trainees to get to know the managers.

☐ The briefing system was changed from a cascade approach, through supervisors, to a direct briefing from the Managing Director and other directors on a quarterly basis.

These changes made some progress in improving communication and heightening the visibility of senior managers, but for many employees the change was relatively minor. While the briefing sessions helped people to feel more involved and valued, the informal grapevine often proved to be a more effective way of finding out about what was happening.

Further, although the visibility of the Managing Director increased, there was still little contact with other senior managers. Any further progress was curtailed when all the changes except the briefings were stopped at the end of 1993. Production had become too busy for the inter-site visits and the Training School was disbanded in favour of on-the-job training.

RESTARTING CI

Key points

- Recruitment of Teaching Company Associates to manage CI.

- Development of a company strategy document to strengthen links between CI and overall company goals.

- Between August and September 1994 all staff were given training which included awareness sessions to improve team-working and to introduce the use of problem-solving tools.

- Five pilot projects, which tackled specific problems, were launched across the different sites and helped to get the commitment and involvement of supervisors.

TEACHING COMPANY SCHEME

The application to the Teaching Company Scheme was successful and in March 1994 two Teaching Company Associates joined the company as 'CI Engineers'. Over the next two years, their task was to guide, facilitate and support the introduction of CI. Instead of the previous steering committee to coordinate the implementation of CI, the CI Engineers reported directly to the Manufacturing Director and attended the monthly Quality Assurance senior management meeting to update the management team on progress.[18] Support and guidance was also provided through regular meetings with the academic Teaching Company Scheme supervisors to facilitate technology transfer from the university to the company.

Initially, the CI Engineers spent some time familiarising themselves with both CI and the operation of the company. The latter involved following a number of products through the

---

[18] Senior management meetings were held every Monday afternoon, with four rotating subject areas: Quality Assurance, Production, Sales and NPD. In addition to the core of the four directors and three functional heads, other key personnel attended according to the subject of the meeting.

organisation, examining information flows across the whole process, from sales enquiry to customer despatch. In the course of informal discussions with managers and other key personnel, they became increasingly aware of a lack of consensus over the strategy and future direction of the company. The strategic direction of the company was represented by 'Target 35', a goal of increasing turnover to £35 million by the end of 1996. This target was to be achieved through three objectives:

☐   improving quality;

☐   improving customer satisfaction;

☐   increasing sales.

However, this broad strategy was not translated into any specific means for achieving the desired growth. As one of the CI Engineers commented, 'Target 35 was a medium-term target, rather than a real strategy'.

Staff questionnaire

In order to clarify further the divergent picture which seemed to be emerging, the CI Engineers conducted a confidential questionnaire survey of all senior managers (around 30 in all) to establish their views on the company's vision, strategy, values and capabilities, and how they saw CI fitting into this. Analysis of the questionnaire responses confirmed a lack of consensus and varying interpretations of the 'strategy'. The circulation of the results caused a degree of surprise amongst the managers, particularly the directors. Consequently, the management team decided to address the issue of strategy.

Developing a strategy and the strategic context for CI

In June 1994, the four company directors, three senior managers and the CI Engineers participated in a one-day strategy session, facilitated by an external consultant. The session addressed the process of strategy formulation and started to explore a number of critical issues within this process. Although the managers recognised that it would take time to develop the detailed strategy, they felt that a more pressing task was to develop a formal statement of the strategic context for CI to support the implementation process and provide a focus. This reflected the agreement that, whatever the strategy, CI would play a key role in its achievement.

Following the session, a CI strategy document was produced, linking CI to the company goal of achieving sustained profitable growth. This growth was to be achieved through two main routes: first through the introduction of new products, technologies and processes; and secondly through the continual improvement of existing products, technologies and processes. The focus for CI was to be on quality, service and delivery. The strategic role of CI was also summarised and communicated through a CI policy statement (Figure 6.2).

> It is the company's policy to continually improve all its products and processes to enhance business performance and create sustained profitable growth. The company recognises that it requires the creative involvement of all staff to implement this policy and has established a set of business processes to enable staff in all parts of the company to participate in the improvement process. The company will enable this activity by providing appropriate resources.

Figure 6.2: *CI policy statement*

CI awareness

The first main step in rolling out CI was to educate all employees in the concept of CI and its role within Hosiden Besson Limited. This was achieved through a series of awareness sessions, consisting of a 45-minute presentation by the CI Engineers and a short exercise to demonstrate the benefits of teamworking. The presentations highlighted what CI would mean for employees, gave an overview of the implementation plan and launched the forthcoming pilots of CI teams. At the end of each session, time was made available for feedback or questions from the participants.

The feedback from these sessions was fairly mixed. Although most people agreed with the concepts behind CI, there was some scepticism as to whether or not it could be made to work at Hosiden Besson Limited. Some people questioned the level of commitment from senior managers and there was some feeling that 'we've not been listened to in the past, so how will it be different this time?'

The bulk of the sessions were run over August and September 1994, in groups of around 20 employees, each comprising a mix of staff from different levels and functional areas. The majority of the workforce attended, although the subsequent growth in the size of the workforce suggested a potential need to carry out further sessions in the future. An introduction to CI was, however, incorporated into the induction training for new recruits.[19]

The importance of winning over the supervisors was seen as a critical factor in minimising resistance to CI. Consequently, a meeting was held with supervisors at the end of October, to update them on progress, explain their role in the CI activity and to support employees, for example, if they came to a supervisor with an idea or if they need to be released to attend group meetings. The attitudes and reaction of supervisors was largely positive, with less opposition than had been expected.

CI process and tools

In parallel to running the awareness sessions, the CI Engineers started developing the process and tools to support the vehicles that were to be introduced, including a CI Process Flow Chart, a Process Improvement/Problem Solving (PIPS) cycle with a user guide, CI procedures and a CI Tool Book. Although the initial CI vehicle was to be formal problem-solving groups, known as CI teams, the process and tools were designed in such a way as to support any CI mechanism irrespective of whether or not it was a team activity, an individual initiative or a one-off meeting to coordinate an activity.

In addition, the CI Process Flow Chart was designed to link CI activities and the Corrective and Preventative Action (CPA)

---

[19] The whole system of induction and training for the shop floor was reviewed by one of the new CI teams.

system. This system dealt with issues raised by quality 'incidents', for example arising from customer complaints, audit failures, supplier failures, customer returns or production yield problems. Linking the two systems would allow CI activity to resolve CPA problems if appropriate (ie PIPS methodology would be used to determine and implement corrective action).

Before the introduction of the pilot CI teams, some of the ideas behind this material were 'tested' in the Surface Mount Technology (SMT) improvement group. This was an improvement group that had been set up in 1993 to tackle efficiency problems in SMT processes – and succeeded in raising efficiency from 30 per cent to around 90 per cent by the end of 1994, and achieving tangible savings of £10,000 per month.

PILOTING THE PROCESS – CI TEAMS

The CI Engineers put together a list of potential projects for the first CI pilots, drawing on a variety of sources, ranging from ideas suggested by employees in the awareness sessions to problems which had been identified by managers. These were prioritised on the basis of a number of criteria, namely:

- □ visibility;
- □ impact;
- □ quick result;
- □ spread (at least one pilot on each of the sites).

Using these criteria, five initial pilots were selected, each to be facilitated by one of the CI Engineers (Table 6.1). The team members were chosen and one member of each team was selected as a team leader, with responsibility for managing the team and ensuring that it achieved its objectives. The team leaders were also required to keep a project folder with notes (decisions and actions) from all the meetings. To help minimise potential problems in the management of the teams, those selected as team leaders were generally in supervisory positions, since they were likely to already have some experience in the running of meetings and were, hopefully, more confident in dealing with people. However, as other employees became more

Table 6.1: *Pilot CI teams*

Team/area	Problem	Solutions	Outcome
Invoice queries	Supplier payments delayed due to invoice queries and invoices sent for approval being held too long	Changed the level of freight charge which can be authorised in Accounts	Average turnaround of invoices for purchasing authorisation within the five-day target set Saving of around two man-days (£150) per month Less friction between Purchasing & Accounts
24A unit	Low efficiency levels on the unit (running at around 30 per cent)	Changed the method of soldering PCB bracket assembly Removed two stages of inspection	Improved quality Reduced throughout time by five minutes per unit (12.5 hours per run)
Audible Warning Devices Packing	Inefficient and costly packing on line	Overtake box holds 50 devices instead of 46 Labelling boxes later in the process Kit storage relocated Equipment relayouts	Easier to count boxes and fewer boxes needed More responsive to customer needs Saving of £48 per month in material and transaction cost, two days per month handling time Improved working conditions and efficiency

Ryde Stores	Problems in the movement of stock shortages from stores to shop floor once they had arrived at the company	Introduced a system for getting urgent production items from loading bays through stores, to production	Average shortage clearance time reduced to 19 minutes Heightened awareness throughout the site of urgent items Expediting resources better targeted
Remote Control Units (Portslade)	Problem with rate of remote control rejects	Use of measurement to identify causes of problem	Reject rate reduced by 90 per cent (exceeding target of 50 per cent reduction)

experienced in group working and the CI process, the selection of team leaders was widened for subsequent projects. The CI Engineers held briefing meetings for the team leaders to explain their role and help instil confidence. The team leaders were given the opportunity to discuss any concerns about their role or the team as a whole. Further meetings were held periodically to discuss any problems which arose.

At the start of each pilot project, team members were given a CI folder and pens (intended as a one-off, for the first time each person participated in a CI team). Each pilot project was allocated an initial budget of £100, to be spent at the team's discretion, although further funding could be made available subject to approval. Records of expenditure were kept by team leaders. At the initial team meeting, the CI Engineers (facilitators) gave an overview of the range of tools, but left out the detailed introduction to the point at which the tool was to be used.

Alternative approaches to tools training were considered but time pressures led to this approach being chosen as opposed to having a more detailed tools training session at the outset. It was also felt that this more gradual introduction might be more effective than 'blinding' people with a detailed tool training session at the start of the project; instead, they would learn how to use the tools more gradually as they reached each successive stage in the PIPS cycle (although this proved not to be the case).

The pilots started in November 1994 and most reached their conclusion toward the end of May 1995. All had achieved significant tangible and intangible benefits. At the end of each project the team members received a CI lapel badge to mark their first participation and a certificate (ongoing for each project). These were presented at a buffet lunch attended by at least one of the directors. At the end of the project the folder was closed and kept in the drawing office for future reference. The outcomes recorded for each project were also collected by the CI Engineers in order to monitor the cumulative benefits of CI activities.

Key outcomes of pilot projects

- Feedback on the learning points from pilot studies were presented.
- Staff were trained as facilitators (18 facilitators have been trained to date).
- New projects were set up and teams were formed to carry them out (47 to date).
- A newsletter and other forms of communication were introduced to support the CI system.

Learning from the pilot projects

The CI Engineers noted some early teething problems in the operation of the CI teams. There were some initial complaints that people were too busy to attend meetings. Following discussions with the senior management team, it was agreed to allow teams to designate a regular weekly lunch-time slot for the meetings, with a buffet provided by the company. In practice, however, there proved to be no demand for the lunch-time sessions; as people began to recognise the value of their improvement activities they were more willing to prioritise time for CI.

Other teething problems were experienced with some of the

team leaders who were uncertain about their role and lacked the confidence to guide the team effectively. Consequently, they tended to lean heavily on the facilitators, particularly in the early team meetings. To overcome this problem, a modular team leader training programme was introduced, which could be geared toward an individual's need. Modules covered the following areas:

☐ project management;

☐ team dynamics;

☐ documentation;

☐ monitoring and measuring;

☐ roles in the team;

☐ overview of team training.

To capture wider learning from the pilot projects, the CI Engineers ran two focus group sessions (April 1995). Two or three representatives from each CI team were invited to attend one of these to feed back on their experiences of teamwork and the CI process. In general, the feedback from the sessions was very encouraging, indicating that much of the initial scepticism had been overcome through participation. Participants had enjoyed the teamwork, felt a sense of achievement and were keen to become involved again in the future. One of the main changes suggested by participants was that they felt the tools and PIPS cycle training would have been more effective if run prior to the start of the project, giving them a better understanding from the outset. Consequently, two half-day training sessions were introduced for team members at the start of a project. The training was intended to satisfy the following objectives:

☐ to give team members a basic understanding of CI;

☐ to explain the benefits of CI for Hosiden Besson Limited and the individual;

☐ to equip team members with the skills to get started on the project;

☐ to allow team members to become familiar with the PIPS cycle and CI tools.

The training adopted a practical and participatory approach, giving people the opportunity to practise using the tools and PIPS cycle.

SELECTING AND TRAINING FACILITATORS

In parallel to the pilot CI teams, preparations were begun to support the wider launch of CI teams by training additional facilitators. A group of around ten people were chosen to train as CI facilitators. In selecting these new facilitators, the CI Engineers looked for people who were enthusiastic, approachable, open-minded and knowledgeable about the company. In addition, all held some position of responsibility, although not necessarily one which involved supervising others. An initial meeting was held with this group as an open forum, to explain the process and their future role as facilitators. Where possible, these employees were included as participants in the pilot teams so that they could start to familiarise themselves with the CI process.

Formal facilitator training was carried out in February 1995 as a three-day course off-site,[20] with the assistance of external consultants.[21] The first day of the training introduced the concepts of CI and put them within the strategic context of Hosiden. It also explained their role as a facilitator. The remaining two days focused on using the PIPS cycle and the associated tools, using a number of interactive exercises to enable a more hands-on approach. The training also covered facilitator skills, including interpersonal skills.

Whilst the facilitators were enthused by the training, there was a general agreement that they did not feel sufficiently confident to start facilitating CI teams. Consequently, it was decided to provide the facilitators with a further opportunity to practise the tools and process by allowing them to work together as a CI team on a live project. The facilitators chose to investigate ways of improving the effectiveness of notice board communications, an issue that had arisen earlier in the training session.

---

[20] Three separate days, each a week apart.
[21] Although it was intended that future sessions would be run internally.

As the first pilot projects were drawing to a conclusion at the end of May 1994, preparations began to launch the next wave of projects to be facilitated by the newly-trained facilitators. Each of these projects was passed through the authorisation procedure, where the project proposal was submitted to a panel consisting of the relevant manager, the potential facilitator and one of the CI Engineers. Proposals that the panel decided were valid as a team problem-solving activity were presented to the Monday management meeting for final approval and to ensure the commitment of the relevant senior manager.

To provide further support for the facilitators, the two CI Engineers adopted a coaching role. Each facilitator also had an individual action plan, one objective of which was to highlight any further training requirements. To heighten their visibility within the workforce, the facilitators were issued with name badges. Having taken into account the learning from the pilots, the first step for the facilitators was to train their team (assisted by the CI Engineers).

Sharing learning and communicating progress

The suggestions for change that emerged from both the facilitator training and the focus groups highlighted the need to incorporate learning mechanisms into the CI process. First, periodic meetings between the facilitators were introduced to allow them to share and learn from each other's experiences. Secondly, a learning feedback form was introduced for the CI teams so that they could reflect upon and record learning from the project.

At the beginning of the pilots a periodic CI newsletter was introduced to update all employees on progress and publicise successes. The newsletter also included some of the problems that teams had experienced to lessen the frustration by showing that people were not alone in facing difficulties. Further, CI updates were incorporated into the Managing Director's quarterly briefings to the whole workforce. Although these proved useful, following the pilots it was decided to introduce further communication mechanisms to facilitate greater learning, namely:

☐   tours of work areas to illustrate improvements to both Hosi-
    den Besson Limited staff and customers;

☐   displaying CI activity through storyboards;

☐   encouraging teams to present their projects to one another
    (optional).

Communication through the company notice boards was also
improved as a result of the CI project undertaken by the facilitator group. There had long been a feeling that the notice boards
were poorly located and untidy, which was confirmed by conducting a survey. Two main changes were introduced. First, two
different types of notice boards were designated, one for company information and one for 'community' information. People
were nominated to look after each notice board (six in total,
across the sites). Secondly, notices were colour coded, categoris-
ing information according to whether it was a company notice,
sports and social, a job vacancy, or health and safety. The new
notice boards were introduced during the summer of 1995.

Toward the end of the first pilot projects, the benefits of CI to
date were collated to produce a summary of achievements. This
was circulated to all directors, managers and supervisors to help
increase awareness of the success and scope of improvement and
to demonstrate the benefits of releasing staff for CI activities.
Managers were also asked to talk informally to those who had
participated to show their gratitude and commitment. The summary of achievements was also communicated to all employees
through the CI newsletter (July 1995).

Senior management commitment

By the end of the pilots, the majority of managers and supervisors appeared to be behind the programme, with the exception
of a few dissidents who had still to be convinced that the scale of
the benefits from the CI teams justified the time and effort
involved. As one manager commented:

> Considering it is only a year on, there has been a lot achieved. I
> was quite surprised actually when I read the newsletter that we
> had attempted and achieved as much as we had.

Problems

However, although senior managers were generally committed, there were some concerns over the lack of visibility of this commitment. Despite encouragement to spend some time walking around the factory and chatting to people informally and to drop in on team meetings, there were few signs that this was happening in practice. There were, however, mixed views from shop floor staff about senior management presence at team meetings. Whilst some felt that this would demonstrate commitment, others thought that the presence of senior managers would upset the team balance. The buffet lunches to celebrate the successful conclusion of a project proved an ideal opportunity for senior managers to recognise the achievements of the individuals who had participated in the CI teams.

These problems, however, do not appear to have significantly affected the levels of involvement and commitment on the shop floor. The fact that people can see real changes being made and that there is a clear organisational commitment reflected in the provision of resources (two full-time staff) have proved to be more important motivators. People recognised that making changes through CI activities ensured that the issues were given greater priority and were therefore easier to push through.

However, for some of the employees who had not been involved, scepticism persisted and they remained to be convinced of the benefits of CI. The level of knowledge and understanding about the changes being introduced under CI was not very high. Information included in the *CI News* was not being reinforced and communicated in others ways – highlighting the need for additional ways of publicising CI. Among those who had not yet been directly involved there was a feeling that little had happened during the year the CI Engineers had been with the company – they had expected to see some activity in their area by now.

Even though a limited number of employees had participated in the initial pilots, by communicating progress and results widespread interest and enthusiasm in CI had been stimulated amongst the workforce. To harness this enthusiasm before it died down, it was decided to start setting up a mechanism for individual involvement (design work started in May 1994). This CI vehicle was called LIFE: Little Improvements From Everyone.

INDIVIDUAL INVOLVEMENT IN CI

Key points

- In late 1993 the LIFE initiative was launched to involve individuals at all levels of the organisation in CI.

- LIFE means Little Improvements From Everyone. The idea was copied from the scheme of the same name at Lucas Diesel Systems (also members of the CIRCA CI Network).

- Ideas submitted by individuals are placed in a visible area of the department, or section, which ensures that they are acknowledged. Feedback is given to the individual if it is not feasible to implement their suggestion. For every idea implemented the company gives a small donation to a local charity.

- The LIFE scheme has been introduced to all areas of the company. At present 400 proposals have been implemented and the quality of ideas is improving all the time.

LIFE

The Portslade site was selected to pilot the new vehicle. A team was set up consisting of supervisors and facilitators. Each member of the team acts as a contact point to whom individuals can come with ideas for improvement. If the contact feels the idea is something the employee can implement immediately by themselves, they are given the go-ahead straight away. Alternatively, they will meet with other members of the team to discuss the idea and decide the most appropriate course of action. Whatever the outcome, this is relayed back to the originator. If they decided that the improvement requires a CI team activity, the idea is put to the proposal panel. For every improvement implemented, £2 is donated to charity.

In mid-1996 the LIFE initiative was introduced to the site at Hove and is currently being launched at Ryde. In general the LIFE initiative has been well received across the company and it has had a positive impact on teamwork, internal efficiency and communication. However, some initial problems arose at Hove. These included conflict between sections, due to the fact that some supervisors encouraged participation in LIFE and others did not. Some supervisors were not convinced that LIFE was a good idea to start with. In order to overcome these problems the Manufacturing Director attempted to convert and convince 'one of the most cynical supervisors' as to the benefits of CI. As a result, others followed suit and were converted to CI. To date over 400 proposals have been implemented, which have had an impact on both large and small issues.

Outcomes of CI initiatives

- Improvement in the quality of goods which has resulted in a lower level of customer returns.
- Reduction in dispatch costs and delivery time to customers.
- Reduction in stock, materials and spare parts held in the factory.
- Improvement in teamwork and cross-functional working (for example, Production Line and Quality Assurance).

FURTHER DEVELOPMENTS

Computer system

At present the company is in the process of developing the new computer system which was introduced in the last year. The new computer system will cover all aspects of the business; for example, sales order processing, purchase orders and stock control.

Quality measurement system

The company is in the process of developing a Quality Measurement System with one of their major suppliers. The system will enable the company to determine the cost of internal failure for critical areas on the production lines across all sites. A programme has been designed that will be issued to operators and used to identify instances of internal failure. The results will be collated on a weekly basis and the cost of 'non-quality' calculated. (The activities which are quality issues have been timed so that a total cost can be estimated.) The measurement system and its purpose has been discussed with operators to gain their support and the establishment of this system is one of the milestones of implementing CI.

DEFINING CI

A set of CI skills have been listed for the Personnel Manager to help identify skills gaps at appraisals and aid in the development of a company skills training plan:

- training and presentation skills;
- problem-solving and analytical skills;
- knowledge of tools and their uses;
- team leader and team member skills;
- facilitating skills;
- knowledge of measuring techniques;
- communication skills;
- knowledge of company systems;
- people skills;
- listening skills.

The definition of CI skills is also intended to help identify potential team leaders or facilitators. The skills would be required in different degrees depending on the role being adopted.

Performance appraisal

In August 1996 a new Performance Appraisal system was introduced which captures issues relating to CI (for example, involvement in CI projects) as well as more general performance

CASE 6: HOSIDEN BESSON LIMITED   169

indicators. The appraisal form has been designed in a short and easy to complete format. The appraisal interview takes place between the staff member and their immediate line manager. Initial feedback seems to suggest that the new system is perceived to be a useful forum for sharing ideas as well as assessing one's performance and should have a strong impact on helping CI to be integrated into general work practices.

Conclusions

The two Teaching Company Associates finished their programme in 1996 and were succeeded by a third Associate, who was employed to help the company to consolidate and advance the CI. CI has led to an improvement in teamworking and sharing of ideas which is being utilised to drive change (for example in developing new products). Efforts are now being made to focus CI activity on overall business objectives and strategy, as well as quality issues.

HOSIDEN BESSON LIMITED – REVIEW OF IMPLEMENTATION

Key points

- Continuous improvement was initially introduced in Hosiden Besson as a means of tackling internal inefficiencies and declining profits.
- The change process was driven by management and supportive personnel, such as the Teaching Company Associates who were employed to manage and coordinate the improvement programme.
- The approach to change was to improve the internal company culture and communication which had been identified, in an external audit, as among the key obstacles to improvement.
- Pilot projects were set up across the different sites which

helped to improve efficiency in the production area, gain commitment among shop floor supervisors and reduce initial scepticism.

■ The company provided formal channels for communication such as a newsletter and the allocation of set times for CI meetings, including the Managing Director's quarterly briefing to all staff which helped to raise the profile of Continuous Improvement. This went some way towards breaking down the 'them and us' climate which had existed.

■ The 'Little Improvements From Everyone' (LIFE) scheme was introduced to encourage individuals to put forward ideas and increase the level of involvement in CI.

Summary

CI has helped the company gain a number of benefits including a reduction in dispatch costs and delivery time to customers, and an improvement in the quality of goods which has resulted in a lower level of customer returns. One of the key internal benefits has been an improvement in teamworking and cross-functional working, for example between Production and Quality Assurance functions.

The company demonstrates an awareness of a number of the key behaviours associated with successful implementation, in particular the need for high levels of management commitment, as well as the opportunity for involvement at all levels. A number of enablers have been put in place to encourage CI, such as the 'LIFE' vehicle and the supportive role of the CI Engineers. The LIFE scheme has now been introduced to all production areas of the company and at the time of writing over 400 proposals had been implemented, with the quality of ideas improving all the time.

However, one of the problems with introducing CI at 'grass roots' level only is that it offers a limited opportunity to link improvement activities to the overall company strategy. As a result CI can operate in parallel to the rest of the organisation, making it more difficult for the change to become deep-seated. In response to this, Hosiden Besson are now in the process of integrating CI into the mainstream company: for example, CI is being incorporated into the new performance appraisal interview and form to help the improvement process become more associated with everyday work practices.

Case 7
TM PRODUCTS
LIMITED

TM Products is located in the south of England and employs around 150 people in the design, production and marketing of products for use world-wide.

OVERVIEW OF CASE

In 1989 FW Talbot Limited was acquired by Thames Water PLC, a privatised utility. In late 1994, Thames Water Products and Services regrouped four separate companies – FW Talbot, Stella Meta, Portacel and Talisman – under the banner of TM Products. Each business has a distinct service and customer base, and products include pipeline products, industrial and portable filtration equipment, disinfection and electronic meter reading equipment.

This case will focus on the Talbot part of the business (formerly FW Talbot Limited), the largest of the units, which is based in Winchester and produces pipeline products. The company has comprehensive facilities for design and sales and marketing, and has a manufacturing policy of components being made by sub-contractors, to the company's quality and design standards. The majority of assembly operations are carried out within the company. Talbot has been the flagship company for continuous improvement and it is now in the process of bringing the other remaining units, Portacel and Talisman (Stella Meta has since been relocated to another part of the parent company) up to the same level.

BACKGROUND

In the late 1980s, FW Talbot realised it needed to improve quality and as a result the company pursued and gained Quality Assurance (BS5750) standards. The company was driven by the desire to improve what it did as a business, not because there were problems, but because it felt that in order to maintain its leading position in the marketplace it wanted to gain a competitive edge by improving customer delivery service levels and lowering its cost base. In late 1991, the company embarked down the path of Manufacturing Resource Planning (MRPII) and Just-in-time (JIT).

In 1993 the company introduced a new computer system as part of its Manufacturing Resources Planning (MRPII) implementation. It aimed to achieve Class A Status (an accreditation of good practice associated with MRPII implementation) by the end of 1994. This process was supported by the introduction of Total Quality Management (TQM).

FRAMEWORK FOR CHANGE

The company used a TQM model, developed by Professor John Oakland, because of its emphasis on customer/supplier links and communication and culture issues (Figure 7.1).[22]

Talbot adapted the model to suit its own needs and a number of quality action plans were articulated to support the change process:

☐ Establish partnerships with key suppliers and develop a programme to introduce quality plans both internally and with suppliers.

[22] John Oakland is the Exxon Chemical Professor of Total Quality Management at the University of Bradford Management Centre. The Oakland approach to introducing Total Quality Management has been used in literally thousands of organisations.

Source: Professor John Oakland

Figure 7.1: *TQM Model*

☐ Manage the MRPII system towards achieving Class A Status.
☐ Ensure adequate training plans are in place covering the management of system hardware and software.
☐ Invest in the training and development of individuals.

BUSINESS EXCELLENCE AT TM PRODUCTS (BEAT) – FORMERLY BUSINESS EXCELLENCE AT TALBOT

In 1992 the company launched a major change initiative under the banner of 'BEAT' (Business Excellence At Talbot), which included three elements: Manufacturing Resource Planning (MRPII), Just-in-Time (JIT) and Total Quality Management (TQM) (Figure 7.2). The company embarked on a major investment in training and an education programme to help encourage the desired change to take place.

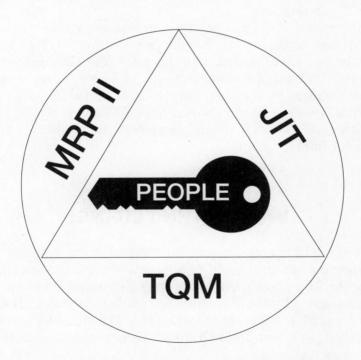

Figure 7.2: *Business Excellence At TM Products (BEAT) model*

MRPII

The MRPII system is a sophisticated planning tool which integrates all aspects of the business through a number of best practice business processes. The system is supported by Just-in-Time (JIT) work practices. JIT is an operating philosophy aimed at eliminating waste in all areas of the business, covering materials, equipment, human resources and capacity.

At a higher level the MRPII system works as an integrated business process to help the company to plan their activities in terms of meeting customer requirements through the successful coordination of a number of activities and functions. The MRPII process involves a high level of communication and tracking of information between different functions. It therefore serves as an appropriate vehicle for highlighting improvement opportunities.

The Sales and Operations Planning process is central to the system and is the driver for determining production capacity, stock levels, supplier and shop floor loading. The process also links into budgeting and business planning, since the forecast of future business in units is converted to sales value and provides a rolling forward view for the business. At Talbot, monthly meetings are held to review the above process, highlighting opportunities for improvement.

IMPLEMENTING CHANGE

In early 1992 a cross-functional support team was set up to organise the integration of MRPII implementation and people elements. The team consisted of the Operations Director, Quality Manager, IT Manager and Materials Controller. Their job was to coordinate the three elements of the change programme (ie MRPII, JIT and Total Quality), recognising the people element was key.

In July 1992 the BEAT initiative was launched companywide and training and presentations were given to all employees outlining the aims of the Business Excellence and Total Quality philosophy. Awareness sessions helped to develop an understanding of the different systems being introduced (such as the MRPII system), as well as acknowledging that the change process brought with it insecurity and confusion which also had to be managed. An Employee Roles Policy was presented, which gave a detailed commitment to developing and training employees.

Impact of training programme

One of the problems identified was that the ideas practised and promoted during training and presentations did not take root as firmly as was anticipated. This was attributed to two causes. First, the BEAT training *preceded* the implementation of the new MRPII system. It was felt that the training took place too close to the MRPII education. Most of the resources in terms of people, time and effort were tied up on the MRPII initiative, which meant that there was little left over to tackle the 'people' side of BEAT which would contribute to the desired culture change. There was also a confusion about the scope of the BEAT initiative: did it represent the more visible technology change, or the softer issues such as culture change? As a result it was seen as something new, rather than as fitting in with existing company aims.

Implementing the new system

In 1993, after a series of pilots, the company cut over to the new MRPII system. The company adopted a 'big bang' approach to implementation rather than introducing the changes gradually, in tandem with existing work practices.

REVIEW OF MRPII IMPLEMENTATION

Three months after the new MRPII and computer systems had been implemented, a review was carried out by members of the

Project Team who had played a key role in supporting the introduction of the new system. The review was based on some of the issues which had arisen during the changeover and what they felt they had learned from them, as outlined in Table 7.1 and Table 7.2.

Table 7.1: *What would we do differently if we had the time again?*

What would we do differently if we had the time again?
☐ Spend more time training system users.
☐ Try understanding more about how the system/company works.
☐ Get a better understanding of the system earlier.
☐ Realise that one cannot work in isolation – working in a team is more effective.
☐ Don't bury ALL the old thinking when introducing change.

Table 7.2: *Learning points from review of MRPII implementation*

Achievements:
☐ Met deadlines, identified critical paths.
☐ Participated constructively in most discussions.
☐ Worked very well as a team.
Learning points:
☐ Increased our understanding of how interdependent the different functions are, and how critical good team-work and communication are.
☐ Reinforced the view that we must work to an efficient formal system at ALL times.
☐ Greater understanding of how the business works – and how we can all work to help each other.

Learning from the experience

The timing of the BEAT launch was unfortunate as the demands of implementing the new system were such that relatively little progress has been made towards CI. The situation could have been avoided had there been a strategic framework within which CI could have been introduced and developed to complement other BEAT activities without being neglected as a result of them. In terms of learning from the experience, the Operations Director said:

With the benefit of hindsight we didn't present a link between where we were then and how we wanted to be in the future. We should have spent more time in workshops and on problem-solving. We had this great presentation and then nothing happened!

Developing a 'shared vision' to support the change process

As part of MRPII implementation a critique was made of the shortcomings of current operations (this was described as 'Company I – The Way We Are Now'). From this arose some issues that could be dealt with immediately, and some longer-term ones which could not be brought about unless the way the business operated was changed. A 'Company II' document was produced – 'The Way We Want To Be' – which showed the confusion gap between business mediocrity (Company I) and business excellence (Company II). This was an interactive process which asked people during the MRPII presentation to come up with things which were wrong with the company at present and to put in suggestions as to how to manage the gap.

Table 7.3: *Bringing about a cultural change*

Company I (Old ways)	Company II (New ways)
Lack of coordinated performance measures linked to corporate objectives	Integrated planning and performance standard
Reasonable customer delivery service	Competitive edge service and on-time launches
Poor inventory record accuracy and physical control	High accuracy and control and capacity planning
Fire-fighting	Controlled emergency action
Untapped individual potential	Employee involvement/development
Need to improve supplier relationships to get more accurate information on capabilities and costs (long lead times and high stock levels)	Supplier partnerships (shorter lead times and lower stock levels)
Computer system creaking and duplication of other software solutions	New computer system/one support solution

Impact of vision

A comparison of the business as it was then (Company I) with the sort of organisation it was aspiring to become (Company II) was followed by major investment in planning and training and education. The creation of a picture of what the company wanted to achieve in the future helped to make some of the problems with the current system more visible. This helped to convince employees across the organisation that the change process was for the best and encouraged them to put all their efforts into ensuring that implementation would be successful. As one person expressed it:

> I was sceptical initially, but I was excited at being part of a company that was taking a risk by implementing a whole new system. My main aim was to work as hard as possible and support my manager to ensure it was a success.
>
> *IT Manager*

BUSINESS IMPROVEMENT TEAMS (BITs)

In 1992 cross-functional teams, called Business Improvement Teams (BITs), were set up. Initial projects involved dealing with the major issues which emerged from the transfer over to the new computer system. Activities included software familiarisation, pilot schemes and the delivery of education and training.

Other BIT projects have since taken place looking at a variety of issues such as packaging, communication problems, reject rates and levels of customer complaints. The value of these teams is that they offered an opportunity to develop cross-boundary working while at the same time ensuring that improvement activities were aligned to the organisation's needs.

The objectives for all Business Improvement Teams were defined at executive level, which ensured that the teams worked on issues that were of strategic importance to the company. The fact that the teams were cross-functional and had members drawn from different levels in the company offered a good opportunity to capture and devolve project learning across the company.

Capturing and Sharing Learning

However, the good practice of having cross-functional teams working on issues of strategic importance was not supported by the use of effective problem-solving tools, and activities tended to be 'reactive' rather than improvement-focused.

A formal corrective action process is documented in the company Quality Manual, and as such is the main problem-solving tool used by teams. The corrective action process is a useful technique for putting things right when they have gone wrong, but is not appropriate for improving processes that are adequate but could be improved.

Although there were clear guidelines around the operation of a BIT, involving ten distinct stages from identifying the issue to receiving a letter of thanks from the Managing Director, there were no mechanisms for capturing and passing on learning – except when a team's activities resulted in a change to an existing company procedure.

A clearly defined learning cycle can help to make effective problem-solving techniques visible and pass on experience and good practice to other teams. Involvement in cross-functional improvement activities through BITs was largely replaced by a more informal process whereby people set up teams as the need arose. This demonstrates a cultural shift, as cross-boundary working now occurs spontaneously as the need arises rather than being driven by a formal process.

TOTAL QUALITY MANAGEMENT

While there was a lot of talk about commitment to quality during the launch of the BEAT initiative, this did not translate into a code of practice which could be shared. The reason for this was that a lot of resources were taken up with implementing the system change and there was little time left over to develop the quality and people side of the BEAT programme.

Encouraging Employee Involvement

One of the aims articulated as part of the 'Company II' vision was to increase levels of employee involvement. The company recognised that a number of mechanisms needed to be put in place to encourage these behaviours, as there was little opportunity for development in the current climate.

Supporting CI through culture change

A range of 'vehicles' including large company-wide, top management-driven projects (lorries), cross-functional teams (vans), departmental teams (cars) and individual improvements (bicycles) were set up to support CI.[23] A CI 'bicycle' known as Kickstart was introduced to encourage people to look for and put into effect small-scale improvements in their immediate work area.

CI Activity Report

A form called the CI Activity Report was introduced, which records and details the improvements made, highlighting any actions that may be useful for other areas of the business to consider. It was hoped that with encouragement, regular reporting and personal recognition the CI process would become self-perpetuating.

Implementing ideas

All ideas had to be reviewed for the potential effects on the company's Standard Quality Procedures (ISO9001) manual. If an idea was at variance with an existing written procedure no change could be implemented without first agreeing the change to the manual with the department manager. Changes outside written procedures could be implemented immediately.

Individual improvement

In the early days of CI implementation a suggestion scheme called 'Bright Ideas' was introduced to encourage people to put forward ideas for change. This involved giving a small monetary

---

[23] The concept of 'CI vehicles' was developed by the CIRCA team at the University of Brighton.

reward, and/or a BEAT mug for good ideas, but this gradually fell into disuse. The managers did not feel that the monetary reward was an appropriate mechanism for encouraging genuine improvement.

The company has moved away from a formal reward system and the level of involvement has dropped in some areas, in particular within Production. Interestingly enough, the standard of ideas has improved since the scheme was abandoned. One of the explanations for this is that people no longer contrive to find problems in order to get recognition, but deal with problems as they arise naturally, through everyday work or by raising them at weekly (or monthly) department meetings.

Review of success

The level of CI involvement varies from one department to another, and the degree to which it is encouraged and supported depends on individual managers. As the Operations Director noted:

> It is naive to expect people to change without leadership. Top management commitment is one of the key attributes for success. The Managing Director has been very supportive of the BEAT philosophy, always willing to take part in education sessions and marketing the concept to his own peers within the organisation.

There are a number of CI champions, including the Operations Director, the Quality Manager and the IT Manager. The IT Department in particular have a high level of involvement in CI. A lot of CI activity takes place informally, which is not captured. The office staff tend to view implementing improvements as part of their job and as a result do not record these changes formally on the CI Activity Report, unless the issues are raised at the department meetings and their manager encourages them to record what they have changed. Again, this highlights the fact that improvements are logged on an erratic basis and levels of record-keeping and encouragement vary from one manager to another.

OPPORTUNITIES TO GENERATE IMPROVEMENT

Opportunities to identify areas for improvement arise as an integral part of the business. For example, at Sales and Operations Planning (SOP) meetings issues are raised around:

☐ Are customer's goods delivered when the customer needs them? What can be done to improve this process?

☐ Inventory record accuracy – are stock levels accurate enough to meet the customers needs? If not, why not and what can be done to achieve greater accuracy?

Meetings

Planning and department meetings and informal team briefings are the key mechanisms for generating improvement activity in the company. According to the Operations Director it is the MRPII process which has had a greater impact on improving performance and culture than CI, as it is a much more visible process and is, therefore, much easier to monitor. For example, if the Sales Department have a problem meeting a customer order it gets picked up and dealt with very quickly.

Process Issue Report

A new mechanism called a Process Issue Report was developed as a means of highlighting areas of the business where improvement is needed but a solution does not appear to be immediately clear. This system encourages people to make their manager or supervisor aware if there is anything that prevents them from performing a work task to the best of their ability. A Process Issue Report can also be used to nominate someone else to sort out the problem. This vehicle is in the early stages of implementation and, as a result, it is difficult to evaluate its success as a means of capturing and sharing opportunities for improvement.

Works Instructions

The company is developing a number of mechanisms to encourage involvement within different areas around the company. In

1996 a graduate student was employed to design and implement Works Instructions in the Production area of the company. These include detailed job descriptions which are used for training new employees and assessing existing staff. The Works Instructions are used to evaluate different skills levels, and assessment is by senior assemblers and trainers as well as an independent person, usually a member of the office staff. A training matrix is used to review standards and a person cannot move to another area until they have passed the skills assessment on their existing work area. The company is currently trying to develop a recognition system which links an internal qualification to different skill levels.

Performance measures

Key performance measures help to drive the business forward and provide opportunities for improvement within the work context. These include:

- Forecast accuracy – the planning of sales to customers.
- Customer service levels, including delivery on time to customers.
- Inventory record and Bill of Material accuracy – measure items on a regular basis.
- Supplier delivery performance and lead time reduction.
- Work order performance – on-time factory completion.

Continuous improvement is driven by performance measures. Everyone knows when something has gone wrong as it gets recorded on the system and, equally, the system can give the projected turnover a month in advance so people have a greater idea of what is expected of them. Performance measures also include customer complaints and levels of sickness and absenteeism. In recent times the company has extended CI to suppliers and to customers. The sales function in particular have contact with the customers and this has led to a greater awareness of customer requirements as well as an improvement in efficiency.

Departmental goals

In the last few years there has been greater linkage between corporate and departmental goals, with less focus on financial targets. By 1995 only one of the company goals was linked to financial targets. The departmental strategies and action plans feed into the goals and targets of individual managers, who pass them on selectively to their employees. In the IT Department the staff try to reach their goals as a team. However, Production team leaders see their objective as remaining under budget against business performance measures that relate to their area and they are not aware of the overall aims of the company.

LEVELS OF RESPONSIBILITY

There is a high level of trust in the organisation, and people at all levels are given a high degree of responsibility. Team leaders in the production area have an input into the employment of temporary staff and they are also consulted on the re-employment of previous staff. It is acknowledged at all levels that the company would 'invest in anything worthwhile which would lead to improvement', and management support the implementation of any positive changes which improve formal work systems and procedures.

An example of the company's freedom to learn approach is demonstrated by the fact that in the early days of the MRPII introduction the Sales function were allowed to experiment and get used to the concept of forecasting while stocks were still high. This helped to encourage people to take risks, experiment and get used to forecasting without having to worry about using up too much stock.

CONCLUSION

We were all thrust into change mode which none of us had experienced before and the main aim was to make people feel part of one group.

Quality manager

The culture of the company is such that in a period of great uncertainty people try to maintain stability. Therefore, it has been the installation of work-related systems such as the new MRPII system which have contributed most to the change process. The system has highlighted the need for greater integration and communication between different functions, which has helped highlight issues for improvement within a work context. The changeover to a new way of working has brought with it changes in behaviour, such as enhancing relations between different departments and listening to each other more to help solve problems.

TM PRODUCTS – REVIEW OF IMPLEMENTATION

Key features

- As a result of the high investment in terms of time and human resources into implementation of the MRPII system, the issues relating to the 'people side' of the change programme were overlooked to a large extent.

- Although the company did not adopt a planned approach to CI implementation, apart from the initial BEAT presentations, the adoption of a shared vision of what they wanted the company to achieve (Company II) helped to focus people's activities.

- An interesting feature of the case is that the core enablers to improvement were those central to the actual business needs rather than any of the ones which were added on, such as the Suggestion Scheme.

- Another interesting point is the way that cross-functional working emerged naturally, as the new systems and work procedures demanded greater liaison and interface between a range of functions.

Summary

In bringing about change the company had not only to deal with the introduction of the new technology system, but also the amalgamation of Talbot with three other business units. As a result there was a desire to create an environment of stability and also make people feel like part of one company while at the same time improving business performance. For the Talbot side of the business the attainment of Class A Status helped to focus people's activities but, as the IT Manager remarked:

> What do you do when you achieve Class A Status, how do you progress and at the same time maintain the momentum?

The company is now in the process of developing a shared work process and culture. In Talbot the MRPII system helped to improve efficiency and communication between different departments and this is the vehicle the company sees as central to their improvement programme in the future.

Recognising that its people are key to its success and the need for top management commitment, the company has identified a number of other attributes for success:

☐ Uncompromising in doing things right.

☐ Involve everyone.

☐ Recognise improvement is not easy, but necessary.

☐ Determination.

☐ Willingness to change.

☐ Establish a culture of honesty and trust.

CI is now being taken seriously at a strategic level in the company. This is demonstrated by a provision for training and the fact that some of the functional objectives in the business plan relate to CI/Total Quality.

Case 8
SCHUNK UK LIMITED

Schunk UK Limited (SUK) is a manufacturing subsidiary of the German based Schunk Group, whose diverse range of products includes sintered metal components and industrial ceramics, carbon products, environmental control products, brush-holders and ultrasonic welding equipment.

OVERVIEW OF CASE

The company introduced CI in 1992 through two formal vehicles (a suggestion scheme and voluntary CI teams) and has made substantial progress in a relatively short space of time, in terms of both tangible savings and cultural change. The adoption of CI forms part of the ongoing development of the business, which started with the implementation of JIT techniques at the beginning of the 1980s and has continued with further change programmes such as the introduction of Statistical Process Control (SPC), manufacturing cells and ISO9002 certification. SUK was the first subsidiary within the Group to implement CI. Its success to date has, however, fuelled a growing interest from other subsidiaries, and a number of employees have visited the site to learn from its experiences.

BACKGROUND

Key points

- Schunk UK founded as a Sales office in London in 1962.
- In 1978 the Sales operation was transferred to Pudsey in West Yorkshire, where production facilities were being set up to supply carbon components to the UK market.
- In the 1980s, Just-in-Time (JIT) and Statistical Process Control (SPC) techniques were introduced due to pressure from customers who had already adopted these procedures.

Schunk UK was founded in 1962 as a London-based Sales office. A production facility was set up in 1977 to supply carbon components to the UK market, and the Sales function was transferred in preparation for the start of production in 1978. In the first year the company employed six production workers and 16 sales and support staff, the majority of whom carried out the trading activities of the old sales office in supplying customers with components produced in Germany. As market penetration increased, turnover from direct production activities increasingly outweighed the trading turnover, as illustrated in Figure 8.1. Although the number of support staff has remained relatively constant, the pattern of growth is reflected by the increased employment within production, from six in 1978 to 58 in 1995 (Figure 8.2). In total, the company employed 94 people in 1995.

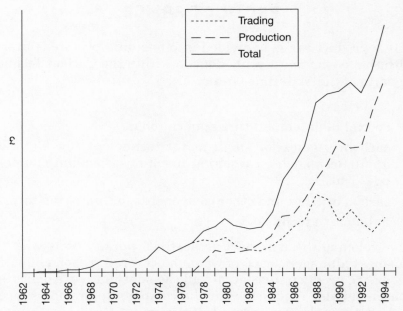

Figure 8.1: *Turnover (trading and production) 1962–1994*

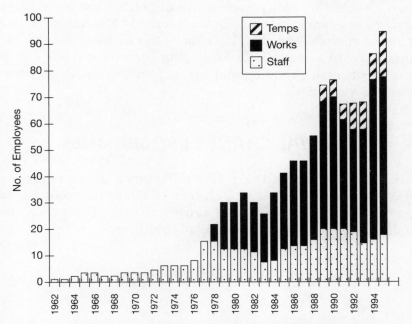

Figure 8.2: *Personnel growth 1962–1995*

PRODUCT RANGE

SUK's product range is divided into five different areas in line with the five business units defined within the Carbon Technology arm of the Materials Group:

☐   seal rings;

☐   special high temperature applications;

☐   carbon brushes for small motor technology (for electrical appliances such as washing machines, vacuum cleaners, power tools);

☐   carbon brushes and other components for industrial motors;

☐   automotive technology.

In developing these product areas, SUK works closely with the Business Managers, each of whom has overall responsibility for one of the product areas across all the subsidiaries. Application specialists also regularly visit the company to provide support and advice in the area of product design.

There are strong lines of control between SUK and the German Head Office. All proposed investments have to be agreed and are incorporated into five-year plans. At the end of the third quarter of each year, SUK produces a 'fine plan' for the year ahead. Twice a year SUK's Managing Director attends a directors' meeting in Germany and once a year the Group Managing Director visits SUK.

INITIAL CHANGE PROGRAMMES

Table 8.1 illustrates the major milestones in the company's development, highlighting a pattern of continual evolution and change. The first major change programme was the introduction of JIT practices at the beginning of the 1980s.

Table 8.1: *Key milestones*

1962	Foundation of Schunk UK
1978	Production started in Pudsey, West Yorkshire
1980	JIT practices introduced
1983	SPC introduced on automotive brushes
1990	BSI certification for ISO9002
1991	Start of kanban deliveries
1993	CI formally launched
1994	Commencement of cell working and pull-through practices
1995	Commencement of Investors in People

As a major supplier to the automobile industry, the company came under increasing pressure from its main customers who were themselves adopting JIT techniques. As customers reduced their raw materials stockholding, typically to one day's worth of component, the buffer of stock that previously stood between them and SUK was virtually eliminated. In order to satisfy customer demands without holding large stocks of finished goods, SUK was forced to change its ways of working and develop the flexibility to cope with the new demands. At the same time, the company started to reduce its dependence on a small number of large customers by broadening its customer base.

The adoption of Just-in-Time (JIT) techniques was followed by Statistical Process Control (SPC) which was again triggered by customer pressure. One customer in particular played a key role in working with SUK in introducing Statistical Process Control which, despite initial difficulties, became an integral part of production, with operators having responsibility for monitoring processes. Manual process control charts have gradually been replaced by computerised versions. As a result of improvements made under Just-in-Time and Statistical Process Control, inspection as a separate function has been largely eliminated (from three people to zero).

The next natural step for the company was to apply for ISO9002 certification. Because of the significant improvements that had already been made and the fact that the company was subject to regular audits from its customers, achieving certification proved to be a relatively easy task, taking around nine months. This was followed by the introduction of a kanban system, both externally, with one of the major customers, and internally. To support the elimination of inspection of goods inward a vendor assessment system was introduced.

INTRODUCTION OF CI

Key points

- CI introduced on an ad hoc informal basis by the Managing Director.

- Designated people appointed to manage a formal CI programme.

- Initial 'big bang' approach to introducing CI in 1993 was followed by more focused small-scale activities concentrating on specific work areas.

- In 1993 a new mission statement was developed which linked CI to the overall strategy and highlighted the pivotal role of staff in achieving these aims.

- A suggestion scheme was set up to encourage individual participation in CI activities.

- In 1994 CI teams were set up, membership of which was voluntary.

At the beginning of the 1990s, Russell Bloor, the Managing Director, started exploring the possibilities of CI. The management literature and the experiences of some of SUK's customers highlighted examples of what could be achieved. Following these examples, the MD instigated a number of improvement activities on an *ad hoc* basis.

This led to a number of small successes which convinced him of the potential benefits. He decided to concentrate efforts on CI and introduce a more formal programme. To lead and coordinate the implementation, he appointed a full-time CI Engineer. Given the size of the company, this represented a major allocation of resources and, therefore, a serious commitment to improvement. The Quality Manager was also closely involved in implementation, particularly in ensuring that CI permeated all activities.

Membership of the CIRCA CI Network also proved helpful in developing an initial implementation plan. This plan identified eight key elements required for successful CI:

1. full management support;
2. a formalised and documented strategy;
3. the whole workforce to be trained in CI techniques;
4. setting up CI teams operating independently on specific problems with the aid of a facilitator;
5. introduction of a company-wide suggestion scheme;
6. a reward system for positive suggestions;
7. regular feedback of progress to all levels throughout the organisation through information boards;
8. a quarterly newsletter.

CREATING AWARENESS

It was decided to go for a 'big bang' approach to CI implementation and introduce all of the major changes simultaneously. Over June 1993, CI training and awareness sessions were used to launch the programme. These were designed and delivered internally by the CI Engineer and run as one-hour sessions for the whole workforce in groups of five. Initially, it was felt to be important to keep these groups as mixed as possible. However, this soon proved to be problematic since a lack of a common language and knowledge base made it difficult to explain the ideas in a way that was meaningful to everyone. Subsequent sessions, therefore, were geared towards similar groups of employees so that the CI concepts could be related to their specific work areas.

The sessions gave an overview of the concepts behind CI, the reasons for its adoption at Schunk and what the company hoped to achieve through its CI programme. This was linked to the new mission statement (Figure 8.3), which highlighted the pivotal role of employees in achieving its aims. The sessions also explained how the new CI vehicles, the suggestion scheme and the CI teams, would operate and the role of a problem-solving cycle and associated tools. The latter was intended largely as an overview since it was felt to be important not to overload people with the detailed tools training at this stage – this would be more effective if introduced as and when people had the opportunity to utilise the tools. Finally, the sessions explained the role of the notice boards and the CI newsletter. At the end of the sessions people were given the opportunity to air their views and raise any questions or concerns. The general reaction and feedback was largely positive.

Schunk UK Limited, the United Kingdom subsidiary of Schunk Werstoff, are committed to becoming a 'world class' company, providing a product which consistently exceeds customers' requirements.

Our objective is to pursue a policy of CI in every facet of the business ensuring that our customers receive the best possible product within the marketplace.

In order to achieve this we recognise that our employees represent the 'lifeblood' and future of the company. The continued success and development of the unit will only be attained if we harness, develop and encourage enthusiasm and involvement of all members of the workforce at all levels.

Training of staff will be continuous, ensuring development of a workforce totally committed to achieving our aims.

Figure 8.3: *Mission statement*

SUGGESTION SCHEME

To encourage greater participation, the suggestion scheme was designed around a very simple form. After writing their idea on the form, employees would then pass it on to the CI Engineer. Initially, the monthly production meeting was used as a forum for reviewing suggestions and deciding subsequent courses of action. However, under this system response times proved to be slow. To speed up response times it was decided to adopt a more informal method of reviewing suggestions, whereby the CI Engineer would consult relevant manager(s) individually to determine whether or not the suggestion was viable. The originator would receive a verbal acknowledgement almost immediately and a written response within seven days.

Irrespective of whether or not a suggestion was to be pursued further, each employee received a written reply thanking them for the suggestion and was rewarded with an hour off work. If the suggestion was not going to be taken on board, efforts were made to ensure that employees received a positive explanation as to why it was not feasible. A further reward of one hour off was made to the best suggestion in any one month. At the end of the first year the originator of the 'suggestion of the year' was awarded a full day off.

Response to the scheme

The initial response to the suggestion scheme was very positive, with 32 suggestions submitted in the first week. However, in the following months the numbers of suggestions have gradually declined, as indicated in Figure 8.4. Between April and August 1995, only two more suggestions were submitted.

In view of the low numbers of suggestions, additional monthly and yearly rewards were abandoned. In total, by August 1995, 90 suggestions had been submitted, of which 31 were implemented, giving an implementation rate of 34.5 per cent. 35 per cent of employees had participated (33 out of a total workforce of 94).

The improvement in response times seemed to have little impact on the numbers of suggestions. A workforce survey[24] revealing a low opinion of the reward amongst employees, may shed some insight into the reasons for the decline. However, the CI Engineer felt that the low participation in the formal scheme did not give a true picture of the real extent of improvement activity since ideas were increasingly being raised verbally through more informal channels. This is discussed later.

[24] Conducted as part of 'Hassle Week'.

The company is constantly looking at new ways to help to encourage people to put forward ideas. The latest scheme was the introduction of a suggestion board with a 'themed' element. Every month the coordinator places a different theme on the board, for example 'savings in raw material', 'bottlenecks' or 'recycling'. Each theme stays on the board for one month. People can put forward suggestions and also see other people's ideas which can help to generate suggestions and help to maintain interest.

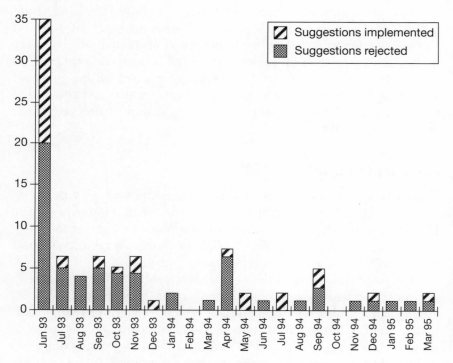

Figure 8.4: *Number of suggestions*

CI TEAMS

The second key vehicle for instigating improvement activity was the CI team. This was a group problem-solving activity whereby a team of employees came together to solve a specific problem.

The first pilot CI teams were set up following the initial awareness sessions, at which employees were invited to volunteer to
participate. From the resulting list, a number of people were
chosen to take part in two pilot projects, each consisting of five
to six people.

Pilot projects

No formal procedures were laid down to guide the operation of
the CI teams. Since the CI Engineer led and facilitated all the
groups, he took on the responsibility for managing the process.
Because of time pressures, the CI Engineer also carried out
much of the investigative role in collecting, measuring and monitoring data to clarify the nature of a problem before putting the
CI team together. Although this limited the involvement of the
team in defining the problem, it minimised the potential strain
on resources which would be created by releasing too many people for a significant amount of time (considerable given the size
of the company). Problems for the groups to tackle were also
selected by the CI Engineer, although the ideas may have origi-
nated from various sources ranging from operators to the Managing Director.

The CI Engineer provided an overview of the seven basic quality tools at the initial meeting. This was not seen as a definitive
training session, however, since the tools were introduced by the
facilitator as and when required. Brainstorming, flow charts,
cause and effect diagrams and list reduction proved to be the
most useful tools. Objectives and targets were set at the beginning of the project and a list of actions generated from each
weekly meeting. At the end of the project all the implemented
changes were recorded and, where possible, the savings quantified. Information from all the CI projects and other improvements were collated in a folder by the CI Engineer.

The mode of implementation depended on the nature of the
solution. As far as possible, the members of the group were
encouraged to implement their solutions themselves. However,
certain solutions required 'expert' input outside the skills of
those in the group, for example, if a machine needed adjusting.

Involvement in CI

By August 1995, 12 teams had been in operation and 39 employees had participated. Membership continued to be voluntary and only one person had declined membership to this date. Responses from employees who had participated were very positive and the extent of savings made by these CI teams was impressive. Figures 8.5 and 8.6 illustrate two projects tackled by CI teams.

Learning points from the CI teams

At the outset it was decided that, as far as possible, the teams should be multi-disciplinary. Although this proved useful in helping to break down inter-departmental barriers, particularly between production and office staff, it hampered the effectiveness of the team, since some of the participants felt unable to make any significant contribution to the problem in hand and other team members had to spend time explaining the basics of, say, a particular production process. For example, one member of the office staff felt that her contribution was limited to providing an objective viewpoint, yet found the experience useful in enhancing her understanding of the production processes. For subsequent projects, although participation continued to be voluntary, the team was formed around those who were most closely involved with the particular subject area.

RESULTS

Some customers were receiving damaged carbon rings. After monitoring the problem, it was identified that the damage was occurring after production, in transportation. The team, consisting of three people, came up with three possible causes of the problem:

1. rough handling by the carrier;
2. inadequate loose fill packing;
3. inadequate protection between each layer of rings.

The third point was dealt with immediately by placing a sheet of cardboard between each layer. At the same time the group experimented with different types of loose fill material. The carriers were invited to Schunk to see if they were able to shed any light on the problem.

The outcome of the project was a substantial drop in the number of complaints regarding damaged rings, from eight in a six-month period prior to implementing changes to one in the same period the following year.

Figure 8.5: *Example of CI team project – packing for carbon rings*

A large amount of scrap was being generated during production of these carbon brushes. The amounts of finished brushes being despatched were much lower than the quantities of raw material that had been originally issued, with an average scrap level of 8.48 per cent. The five members of the team set an initial target of reducing scrap to 5 per cent.

Thirteen possible solutions were generated and list reduction used to identify the main ones, which were related to the inefficiencies in the scales used to count the brushes:

1. Secure the bench on which the scales were mounted to the wall.
2. Place the scales within a frame mounted on the bench top to make them less prone to movement.
3. Record all setting scrap.
4. Have pellets delivered in boxes instead of bags to reduce the risk of losing pellets during transit.

Having implemented these, the discrepancy between the quantities issued and the quantities despatched fell to an average of 0.9 per cent, well below the original target.

Figure 8.6: *Example of CI team project – Black & Decker '457' carbon brushes*

PROBLEM-SOLVING CYCLE

Following the pilots, adjustments were also made to the problem-solving cycle itself. The initial cycle, which had been 'borrowed' from one of their customers proved inappropriate for the team activity at Schunk since it had been customised to suit the specific needs of the customer. Consequently, a more standard, generic cycle was adopted. To support the problem-solving cycle, details of each of the tools were written up and collated in a folder as a toolbox. This was made available to employees by pinning copies on the notice boards.

COMMUNICATION MECHANISMS

Two new communication mechanisms were introduced to support the introduction of CI. First, a number of notice boards were set up, two on the shop floor and one in the offices, to promote company-wide information sharing. The boards were used to display a range of information, including:

☐   overall company performance data, such as internal and external defect levels;

☐   figures on the level of absenteeism;[25]

☐   letters from suppliers (both positive and negative);

☐   details of forthcoming visitors to the company.

This last has proved particularly useful. Prior to the establishment of the notice boards, if employees saw visitors being taken around the factory, they would rarely have any idea who they were. Blank forms for the suggestion scheme were also attached to the notice board. Feedback indicated that the majority of employees found the boards useful and relevant. There were, however, additional demands for more department-specific information.

The second communication mechanism introduced was a quarterly company newsletter which aimed to keep employees

---

[25] To encourage low absenteeism, employees who had no days absence other than holidays in 1994 were rewarded with a Marks & Spencer or Asda voucher worth £15.

informed about developments within Schunk UK and across the group as a whole. It included information on, and an explanation of, the company's financial performance and major developments at SUK and other Schunk subsidiaries. Previously, employees had received very little information about the group as a whole. A section of the newsletter was devoted to CI and quality news to update on progress in these areas. Efforts were also made to include social information, which was popular amongst employees, although some encouragement was needed to persuade people to put this information forward. Initially the newsletter was pinned to the notice board. However, it was soon realised that few people were actually bothering to read it. Consequently, copies were made available in the canteen area.

PROGRESS AND PROBLEMS

Key points

- Opposition was initially experienced at management and supervisory level. However, these fears were soon allayed as the benefits of CI began to show through.

- While there was a noticeable drop in formal participation in the CI suggestion scheme it soon became apparent that people were volunteering ideas on an informal basis.

- Reorganisation into manufacturing cells helped to foster a CI culture and gave operators greater control over their work.

The pace of change within SUK has been quite quick and there is some feeling that perhaps they have been trying to change the organisation too rapidly.[26] However, few problems have been experienced in gaining the involvement and commitment of employees, aside from some initial fears that CI was primarily a cost-cutting exercise that would possibly lead to job losses.

---

[26] The reorganisation into manufacturing cells took place at the same time as implementing the CI programme.

These fears were soon allayed as redundancies did not materialise and, in fact, the size of the workforce started to increase after the adoption of CI.

More significant opposition was initially experienced at management and supervisory levels. In part, this reflected a reluctance to change when the company was performing relatively well – 'we're doing all right so why do we need to change?' Further, some saw CI as a threat to their own position as activities were being undertaken by the quality and CI staff which would previously have been carried out by them. The foreman felt that these problems could have been minimised by making more effort to involve managerial staff from the outset. The importance of winning the support of these people was recognised and attempts made to address the problem by working more closely with them. Opposition was also further eroded as the cumulative benefits of CI started to emerge. However, some problems were still experienced in releasing people from production to participate in CI teams due to time pressures.

As mentioned earlier, one of the main problems experienced was a sharp drop in formal participation in CI through the suggestion scheme. At first glance, this seemed to indicate a decline in the momentum of improvement activity. However, it soon became apparent that the level of savings was being maintained due to an increase in informal activity. People seemed to feel more comfortable raising ideas verbally with the CI Engineer than submitting them as formal suggestions. Thus a more participative culture was starting to emerge, whereby employees were becoming more independent and more willing to question things and share ideas. CI had contributed toward the development of a 'blame-free' culture where people were encouraged to discuss problems and identify how these could be prevented in the future. The CI Engineer felt that the belief in the value of small improvements was becoming increasingly widespread. Through the new channels of communication, the working environment was becoming more open, reducing the 'us and them' barriers.

Developing a CI culture

Improvement in communication and manager-employee relations was also enhanced by the relocation of the offices of the Quality Manager, CI Engineer and Production Manager to the centre of the factory floor. In addition to making managers more visible, the open door policy adopted by these managers made them more approachable, since employees were able to consult them with any problems or queries as they arose.[27] Single status (which involved treating all staff equally) was also promoted by introducing overalls and company T-shirts for all Production-related staff, irrespective of seniority.

Increased empowerment was further supported by a major reorganisation of production into manufacturing cells, which introduced a more logical, streamlined structure. The reorganisation into manufacturing cells has further embedded the notion of teamworking. Each cell has a designated 'spokesperson', chosen by the group (who can be deselected as they see fit). These provide a focal point for contact between the Factory Manager and the operators in the cell. Every Monday morning the cell leaders meet with the Factory Manager and Foreman to be briefed on the week's production and discuss any outstanding or potential problems. This information is relayed back to the other workers in the cell who then organise themselves and the machines to meet the production requirements. The reorganisation, therefore, leads to operators having greater control over their work. Multi-skilling is also encouraged where possible. As one cell leader commented,

> The atmosphere has changed now. You feel more part of a group and the organisation has become more open.

The improvements were not only visible to those within the organisation, but were also commented on by visitors to the factory.

Changes in the internal organisation were reflected in a new organisational chart (Figure 8.7) which replaced the old hierarchical organisational chart. It was felt that the formal structure represented in the old chart did not reflect the interrelationships between different areas, nor the range of links between internal personnel and the external customers.

[27] The office relocation also freed up a room, away from the shop floor, to act as a meeting room where training sessions can be run and CI teams can meet.

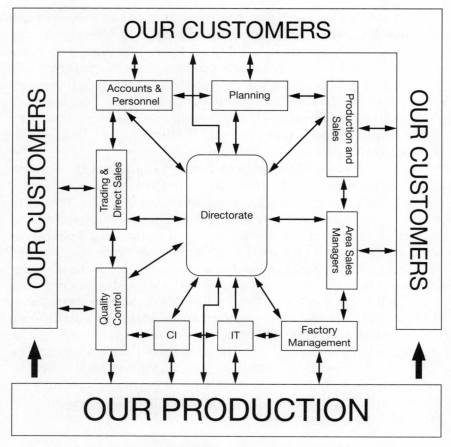

Figure 8.7: *New organisational chart*

Employee questionnaire

In October 1994, all employees were given the opportunity to feed back their views on the various elements of the CI programme, the working environment and their levels of job satisfaction. A questionnaire was sent out to all employees, under the banner of 'Hassle Week' – so-called because it gave employees the opportunity to put forward anything that was a 'hassle' about their work. The questionnaire achieved a 50 per cent response rate. The results were published and made available to all employees. This indicated that, generally, attitudes were fairly positive, particularly in relation to the safety of the working environment, having a good understanding of how the operations they perform affect both internal and external customers, and the availability of equipment to carry out work effectively. Levels of job satisfaction and the approachability of managers also scored fairly well. The survey did, however, indicate that employees still felt there was an 'us and them' culture between the office and shop floor staff.

The main problems raised were relatively minor:

☐ lack of social news in the newsletter;

☐ lack of department-specific information on notice boards;

☐ inadequate reward system for the suggestion scheme;

☐ lack of information supplied to the night shift.

INVESTORS IN PEOPLE (IIP)

In 1995, the company registered a certificate of intent for the IIP scheme and underwent an initial assessment by external consultants to identify what changes were needed to achieve IIP status. Following this, a project plan was developed spanning 18 months and incorporating the following stages:

☐ induction training;

☐ strategic people plan and training policies;

☐ appraisal design and training;

☐ conducting appraisals;

☐ management skills definition, audit and training;

☐ target- and standard-setting process;

☐ portfolio preparation;

☐ IIP assessment.

The above changes were seen very much as being complementary to the CI programme. Consequently, the CI Engineer and the Quality Manager were given overall responsibility for the project, and they liaised closely with the Managing Director and the Personnel Assistant. As at August 1995 the first two stages of the plan, induction training and the strategic plan, had been

208 CONTINUOUS IMPROVEMENT IN ACTION

completed and work had started on developing an appraisal system (initially for office staff as a pilot).

The strategy was based upon the following objectives:

☐ to be profitable;

☐ to provide a good working environment;

☐ to develop people to the best of their abilities;

☐ to grow;

☐ to provide a secure future for employees.

Each of these objectives was then broken down into specific goals and tools for achieving them, with CI playing a key role. The process of developing and communicating this strategy helped to demonstrate the active commitment of the Managing Director, who communicated the strategy to all employees through small group sessions of around 12 people. Each presentation was followed by open 'question and answer' sessions, where employees were given the opportunity to ask any questions about the business.

The induction training was designed and delivered by the CI Engineer and lasted around one hour. The session covered areas such as CI, ISO9000 and health and safety. In addition, a machine checklist was put together to help new recruits, outlining operating procedures and other notes for each machine.

Summary of outcomes to date

The turnover and personnel growth (Figures 8.1 and 8.2) highlight the continued growth of the company. However, in view of the relatively short time since CI was adopted and the other various changes that have taken place over the same period, it is difficult to attribute such trends directly to CI activity. However, the tangible savings accruing from CI had been documented since 1992. By August 1995 the total savings amounted to £211,854. It should be noted, though, that this figure understates the full extent of the quantified benefits since each saving is counted as a one-off amount irrespective of whether or not the saving will continue to be realised in subsequent years. For example, the relocation of a machine saved £840 per year. This was included in the total as £840 whereas by the end of 1995 the actual saving would have been three times that, ie £2520.

Figure 8.8 also suggests that CI is likely to have a significant impact on internal efficiency. The potential turnover lost reflects the cost to the company of production defects and making other errors in terms of the money they would have received for an item had a problem not arisen, ie failure is recorded in terms of the selling price of the item. The figure indicates that between 1993 and 1995 there has been a significant fall in the amount of potential turnover lost.

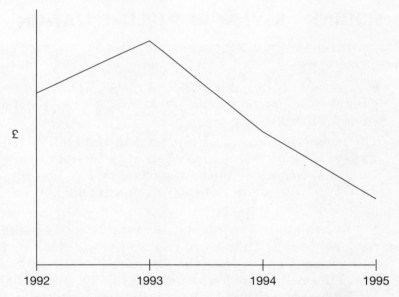

Figure 8.8: *Potential turnover lost by production defects*

CONCLUSIONS

To date, the CI programme has been successful and the majority of employees seem happy with it. Over the years people have joined in groups and also workshops where they can learn how to use CI tools such as brainstorming and Pareto analysis, as well as having the opportunity to contribute ideas and become involved in decision-making. Within the CI groups everyone is given the opportunity to air their own views without the fear of reprisal, and over the years this has helped to gain support for CI as well as increasing the level of trust within the organisation.

Most people perceive CI as an opportunity to contribute towards their own personal development and work closely with other people. As CI is an ongoing process it ties in with the future developments in Investors in People and both processes should help to increase the level of learning which is taking place both formally and informally within the organisation.

SCHUNK – REVIEW OF IMPLEMENTATION

Key points

- CI was initially introduced at Schunk UK when the company decided to use its BS5750 standard as a stepping stone for further improvement.
- The company recognised the need to change internal ways of working and improve flexibility, in order to cope with new demands. Among the changes was the introduction of cellular working in manufacturing and total production maintenance.
- Whilst Schunk UK operated in accordance with existing corporate plans they were free to pursue their own improvement plans. However, the parent company was kept informed of progress made and their success has fuelled a growing interest from the other subsidiaries of Schunk.
- Although initial CI activity was linked to small-scale improvements, the programme evolved quite rapidly to incorporate more strategic objectives. The CI mission statement highlighted the key role of staff in achieving the strategic aims and this helped people feel they had a part to play in the change process.
- A lot of changes took place at the same time, for example the reorganisation into manufacturing cells occurred concurrently with the implementation of Total Produc-

tion Maintenance. Nevertheless, few problems have been experienced in gaining employee commitment. Initial fears that the new ways of working would result in redundancies did not materialise and this contributed to the high level of support and involvement among shop floor staff.

■ The relocation of key support managers to the centre of the factory floor, as well as the adoption of an 'open door' policy for management, helped improve communications and reduce the 'them and us' culture.

Summary

The process of change at Schunk made rapid progress over a short period of time. One of the key success factors was the 'organic' approach which resulted in changes in work practices and the way physical work space was used that helped to bring shop floor and management staff together. This helped to improve communication and resulted in an increased level of trust in the company.

The fact that Schunk UK is a reasonably small organisation with 90 staff in total was, perhaps, one of the reasons why the changes had a large impact early on. People perceived CI as an opportunity to contribute towards their own personal development and work closely with other people.

By including some suppliers in the programme the company has strengthened the impact of CI, linked activities to overall aims and helped to make CI an integral part of everyday life.

One of the main learning points from this case is the way the company managed cross-boundary working and training. Team activities helped to share learning and capture the view points of 'objective outsiders', while training was delivered to people from a common function and knowledge base to ensure that the training and concepts remained meaningful.

The Schunk case is a good example of how continuous improvement can be implemented with a high degree of success in an organisation which is a subsidiary of a larger company.

SUMMARY AND CONCLUSIONS

In the concluding chapter, we examine some of the general themes emerging from the case-book and explore how they contribute to a broader understanding of CI in action. The findings from the individual cases are also illustrated, in particular regarding the enablers which helped to support implementation, some of the companies' learning points and the problems faced. Finally, we sum up with some generic points which help contribute to an understanding of good CI practices.

BENEFITS OF CI

All of the case studies outline some good examples of the benefits which can arise from CI, both tangible gains such as cost savings and intangible benefits, for example, improvements in employee relations and customer service.

In particular, cross-functional teamworking has helped to break down some of the barriers between different departments within companies.

Programmes which aim to integrate different functions, such as design and manufacturing at BAe, and the project at Veeder Root which involved internal and external (off-site service engineers) employees in the development of testing equipment for faulty goods, are good examples of such cross-functional working.

Advantages the case companies gained from the application of CI include the following:

- **Significant financial benefits** resulting from better use of human resources and more efficient and target-focused work practices through the use of methods such as Just-in-Time and Policy Deployment.

- **Greater communication** and cross-boundary working (both internally and externally) which in many cases has improved the company culture and contributed to greater flexibility in meeting customer demands.

- **Improved vertical communication** across the different levels within the organisations.

- **More visible management** and stronger management commitment which has helped to break down traditional 'them and us' barriers.

- **Strategic benefits** such as improved customer satisfaction which has contributed towards a rise in profits and increased competitive advantage.

- **Improved awareness and understanding of the company's overall business aims** and also the mechanisms they are using to achieve them.

- **Culture change** through the use of improved methods of evaluation and assessment has contributed to development and learning within the organisations.

- **Increased involvement** in improvement activities.

- **Improvement in processes** such as a greater understanding of individual roles and job responsibilities within the overall business aims.

- **Rigorous correction procedures** and the use of effective review and reporting systems.

COMMON FEATURES OF CI IMPLEMENTATION

The cases also demonstrate a wide range of experiences and approaches to implementation. However, there are a number of underlying themes. Here is a summary of the key similarities and patterns to implementation.

- The eight companies all adopted CI in response to pressure, either from **external sources** such as customers or due to a realisation that the company was suffering from **internal inefficiencies**.

- In a number of cases, the rationale for CI introduction was driven by one or more members of the **management team**.

- The initial implementation involved a reorganisation of working practices, in particular within **operations**. An example is the adoption of a task-focused approach, involving changing and expanding job roles, such as that which took place at NPI and Lucas Diesel Systems.

- Increased levels of responsibility and job enrichment were also a key feature of early changes. In manufacturing sections, there appeared to be a common trend to **move towards more process-oriented ways of working** through reorganisation into manufacturing cells, product streams and also by encouraging cross-functional working.

- The above changes to ways of working, both in terms of **physical changes** to the work unit and also of **work content**, helped to achieve greater levels of productivity, improve individual autonomy and increase understanding of, and adherence to, quality standards. The changes also aimed to improve teamworking within teams and across the organisation, as well as increasing overall levels of involvement and innovation.

- Another organisational change which took place in the companies was **restructuring the organisational hierarchy** to make it flatter. This helped reduce the number of bottlenecks and levels of authority between the different employee grades.

- **Team meetings and suggestion schemes** helped give individuals and teams a greater feeling of control as well as encouraging communication and creativity.

DEVELOPMENT OF CI

As already noted the companies faced different challenges in the early days. Some, such as Fortes Bakery, focused on culture changes and others, such as TM Products, concentrated on technology changes. These examples show that the order in which different issues are tackled will depend on the individual circumstances of the company. However, a company that introduces system and structural changes by either simplifying or improving a process needs to create an environment where people can make meaningful contributions. Examples include the introduction of a new 'craftsperson' grade at Lucas Diesel Systems and the provision of a Company Open Learning Centre. At NPI, front-line staff were given training to equip them with the skills to improve customer satisfaction and develop enhanced working relationships with the customers.

Enablers used to encourage CI activity and help focus on the organisation's objectives include setting targets, devolving responsibility and utilising customer feedback – as a means of ensuring CI flourishes and remains linked to the organisation's overall objectives.

SOME COMMON FEATURES IN CI

While the type of CI programme is contingent on individual organisational needs, the case studies demonstrate a number of common basic features in terms of the companies' initial approach to CI and what they hope to achieve from it.

☐ CI was often introduced to internal functions/operations as a reaction to internal inefficiency and declining competitiveness.

☐ The companies' initial programmes were directed towards, and made an impact on, production/operations and, in the case of NPI, front-line staff.

☐ Identification of the factors which supported organisational development – in particular teamworking and cross-functional working – and putting in place enablers to support the growth of these behaviours. Examples of enablers include team briefings to aid communication, and structures to encourage involvement such as project teams and suggestion schemes.

The companies which developed in terms of CI tended to adopt a planned approach to change which included getting rid of any systems or procedures which were surplus to organisational needs or were simply no longer of value and created excess work. Examples include overly bureaucratic communication or paper-based systems that created extra work. Building on this 'weeding out of surplus', the more advanced CI programmes then rolled out the initiative to capture other areas of improvement.

☐ Companies which evolved to higher levels of CI have managed to build strategic aims into CI, through changing work roles which helped the changes to become embedded in the culture and offered genuine opportunities for improvement. Embedding CI in work practices and giving a real opportunity for employees to see results quickly helped to increase the impact and profile of CI.

☐ Some more advanced companies have managed to build on CI achievements and spread the impact of activities by including stake-holders, such as suppliers and customers, in a mutually beneficial improvement programme.

RECOGNITION

Many of the companies have moved away from monetary rewards and, interestingly enough, have found that the standard of ideas has improved – as the ideas are motivated by genuine recognition of a problem rather than just seeking reward. Some of the companies have rejuvenated their recognition systems in order to sustain interest and momentum. Many companies have also recognised the value of simply saying 'thank you' which, according to employee feedback, seems to be particularly motivating.

MANAGEMENT COMMITMENT

In order to demonstrate their commitment to improvement activities, managers had to be both flexible and innovative. An example of this in practice is provided by the managers at NPI who walked around wearing sandwich boards on which people were encouraged to paste suggestions about how to improve empowerment and recognition in the company! Some less dramatic instances include the occasion when senior management at Hosiden Besson worked alongside employees on the production line in order to fulfil orders during a time of immense production pressures, and the commitment by Fortes Bakery to develop a more effective style of management.

BARRIERS TO IMPLEMENTATION

The cases show some good examples of management commitment to CI. However, the role of management was, in general, to guide and support CI rather than to be actively involved in the process. This appears to be particularly true at senior or management team level. While some managers appeared to be able to drive and endorse CI in other areas of the company, the biggest problem was often gaining real commitment and support from their own peers.

Some difficulties were identified around the use of enablers. A commonly cited problem was that learning had not taken place and that people were not naturally using the problem-solving tools. Some of the cases also identified that the methods of sharing communication were not always effective.

Company-wide CI presentation events which pay homage to CI can often leave those who have not been involved in a project feeling left out and resentful. Unless there is provision for employees to ask questions or give feedback the exercise can simply serve as a corporate presentation. One of the most effective means of communication identified by the cases is the use of the team briefing system, which can also be a useful forum for capturing and sharing learning and progress.

SOME CI ENABLERS

☐ **Support from senior management** in terms of resources, commitment and leadership.

☐ **Pilot projects** to give the opportunity to try out new ideas and experiment; for example HBL and TM Products.

☐ **Assurance that CI will not lead to job losses**, which is a major factor in hindering motivation and innovation.

☐ **Clear and consistent messages from management**; no false promises (for example at Schunk).

☐ **Meaningful opportunities to try new skills** linked to actual work practices (such as at BAe).

☐ **Encouragement of cross-functional working**.

☐ **Use of different methods of measurement and benchmarking** to evaluate progress and learn from mistakes.

☐ **Timely and relevant use of training and problem-solving materials**. Most of the companies seemed to become aware of the value of timely and relevant training, for example by addressing groups of employees with similar job-related knowledge when teaching job-relevant skills, and using cross-functional groups when teaching broader lessons, such as those related to organisation-wide, rather than departmental issues.

☐ CI not introduced and maintained as a parallel system but **integrated as a key part of work processes and organisational objectives**.

☐ CI linked to strategy at all levels, for example, through **target-setting, policy deployment and a clearly understood mission statement** which offers the opportunity for involvement at all levels.

☐ **Opportunities for all levels to become involved in CI** without forcing changes unnecessarily – or expecting them to change too quickly.

☐ **Measurement and benchmarking** play an important role in evaluating progress and planning future CI initiatives.

☐ **Regular feedback** to monitor and manage the programme can also help to iron out any problems and ensure CI is focused on issues of priority to the organisation.

☐ **Strong and visible leadership.** 'Practice what you preach' is a strong message from the case studies and also helps to break down the often-reported 'them and us' barriers between management and employees.

LEARNING FROM EXPERIENCE

The eight cases in this book demonstrate that the introduction of CI is not automatic or straightforward and that often a company can only progress following a period of unexpected or disappointing outcomes, which cause a refocusing of the activity and a renewed look at what the initiative is trying to achieve.

☐ After the initial introduction, and use of consultants, Fortes Bakery developed their own CI agenda and terminology and all training was delivered in-house by managers, rather than using consultants.

☐ At Veeder Root, Policy Deployment was identified as the main activity for both continuous improvement and meeting company business aims. As a result, a Policy Deployment Matrix was developed which devolved responsibility for meeting business targets to all levels within the company.

☐ Initial feedback at BAe showed that employees were suffering from CI overload. As a result the company developed a strategic policy which classified and prioritised projects according to their importance and relevance to the overall business aims.

☐ At Schunk UK, initial efforts were focused on improving manufacturing processes and later initiatives concentrated on developing people to the best of their abilities under the IIP initiative, which was identified as a key objective for the company.

REVIEW

These examples taken from the case studies give some useful lessons in CI practices, as well as offering practitioners a framework in which to introduce, or evaluate, their own CI programmes. From the cases it is evident that CI offers a number of benefits if properly implemented, both in terms of cultural change and tangible savings.

The problems encountered during CI implementation often result from adopting a superficial approach to the change process, not taking a long-term plan, and not involving key personnel in the process.

These findings suggest that CI is not merely a series of enablers and mechanisms, although these are fundamental to driving and supporting change. Rather, CI is about developing new ways of behaving and sustaining them in the long term to bring about significant organisational advantages.

One of the key learning points the cases demonstrate is that CI needs to offer a chance for meaningful involvement at all levels in order for it to become ingrained in the culture and have a widespread impact on the business and the people as a whole. As Hugh Chapman, Site Director at Veeder Root expressed it:

> CI looks at any aspect of our business to try to make small improvements, which helps keep our attention focused on everything. We need to make modest gains, going back to the drawing board, and looking forward all the time.

The case stories suggest that the companies are becoming more outward-looking and using forward planning in their approach to CI. Many focus on measuring company-wide performance, for example through external and internal benchmarking procedures, project management and by using self-assessment techniques such as the European Foundation for Quality Management model, which was used in some of the case companies.

Above all, the cases related here reinforce the view that there is no secret ingredient to introducing CI. They demonstrate some of the practical steps companies can take to help CI to become an integral part of organisational life and ensure that it will not fall at the first hurdle.

BIBLIOGRAPHY

Introduction

[1] Bessant, J and Caffyn, S (1997) 'High involvement innovation through continuous improvement', *International Journal of Technology Management*, vol 14, no 1, pp 7–28.

[2] Schroeder, DM and Robinson, AG (1991) 'America's most successful export to Japan: continuous improvement programs', *Sloan Management Review*, vol 32, Spring, pp 67–81.

[3] Robinson, A (ed) (1991) *Continuous Improvement in Operations: A Systematic Approach to Waste Reduction*, Productivity Press, Cambridge, MA.

[4] Imai, M (1987) *Kaizen: The Key to Japan's Competitive Success*, Random House, New York.

[5] Lillrank, P and Kano, N (1989) *Continuous Improvement – Quality Control Circles in Japanese Industry*, University of Michigan Press, Ann Arbor, MI.

[6] Caffyn, S and Silano, M (1998, in press) 'Continuous Improvement in the UK' in *Continuous Improvement in Europe and Australia* (Berger, A, Boer, H and Gertsen, F, eds).

[7] Bessant, J, Caffyn, S, Gilbert, J, Harding, R and Webb, S (1994) 'Rediscovering Continuous Improvement', *Technovation*, vol 14, no 1, pp 17–29.

[8] Caffyn, S (1997) 'CIRCA Continuous Improvement Self-Assessment Tool' (version 3), copyright Centre for Research in Innovation Management at the University of Brighton.

Case chapters

Bicheno, J (1991) *A Guide to 8 Gurus, 7 Tools, 7 Wastes, 12 Techniques*, PICSIE Books, Buckingham, UK.

Blackstone, CJ and Brookes, NJ (1996) *Concurrent Engineering, What's Working Where*, Gower Publications Limited.

Brown, S (1996) *Strategic Manufacturing for Competitive Advantage, Transforming Operations from Shop Floor to Strategy*, Prentice Hall, UK.

Ciampa, D (1992) *Total Quality*, Addison-Wesley Publishing Company, Reading, MA, p xxi. Cited in French, WL and Bell Jr, CH (5th ed, 1995) *Organizational Development, Behavioural Science Interventions for Organization Improvement*, Prentice Hall Inc.

Hoffman, K and Kaplinsky, R (1992) 'The Experience of Lucas LFS, Transitional Corporations and the Transfer of New Management Practices to Developing Countries', *Case Studies of Organisational Change in an Industrialised and Semi-Industrialised Economy*, pp 54–74.

Imai, M (1987) *Kaizen: The Key to Japan's Competitive Success*, Random House, New York.

Loveridge, R (1988) 'Lucas Industries, A Case Study in Strategic Domain and Discourse', University of Aston, UK.

Loveridge, R (1989) '"Footfalls of the Future": The Emergence of Strategic Frames and Formulae', in *Strategic Management and Technological Innovation* (Loveridge, R and Pitt, M, eds), Wiley & Sons, Chichester.

Sashkin, M and Kiser, KJ (1991) *Total Quality Management*, Ducochon Press, Seabrook, MD.

Taylor, P and Thackwray, B (1995) *Investors In People Explained*, Kogan Page, London.

INDEX